First Published July 1995
Revised and Reprinted February 1996
Revised and Reprinted September 1996

By the same author:
Sunshine and Showers

Reflections
and
Dorset Recollections

A Book of Thoughts, Memories and
Anniversaries
for each day of the year

by

MAURICE S. ENNALS

Illustrations by Felicity Ann Larard

ISBN 0 9519771 4 8
Telwoth Books, Dorset DT2 8AB

Printed by
Creeds the Printers, Broadoak, Bridport, Dorset DT6 5NL

Foreword

This little book is full of bits of wisdom, good thoughts, poems and other kindly odds and ends. Maurice Ennals has put them together with obvious enjoyment, and I am sure that reading them will give to many the same enjoyment.

Leslie Thomas

Salisbury

Preface

As we travel along life's busy highway all of us, at some time or other, search for the green pastures – to be 'alone with ourselves', as someone once put it. When we discover such rare and precious moments, some of us turn to music. Others turn to writing, others to reading; others spend their time in quiet reflection.

This book is meant for those who prefer to read – and to reflect. Although each item is chronicled against a date, many with special significance to that date, it is a book for all seasons, all occasions, to be picked up, perused, and laid down as one's mood dictates.

Much of it is centred on life in Dorset, living as I do in this beautiful county with my wife and most members of our family; but I have not allowed this to influence unduly my choice of subjects – these reach well beyond any geographical boundary. Great names, profound sayings, simple truths, historic anniversaries, homely anecdotes . . . All are here to stir our memories – some glad, some sad, some amusing.

Considerable research has gone into the writing of the book. My reward, after two years' work, was to see *Reflections* at last completed, checked and ready for the bookshelf. I hope, dear reader, your reward will be the peaceful pleasure you derive from turning the pages – and reflecting.

Every seven days or so, you will find a quotation from The Good Book. I have selected these from the King James version because I believe it is still the best loved, and best known, of all translations. Where possible, the quotation is appropriate, or at least not inappropriate, to the date against it and/or the subject immediately preceding it.

Following the successful sales of the first edition of

Reflections, the book has now been revised and reprinted twice, with some additions and minor amendments.

I should like to express my sincere gratitude to my dear wife, Kay, for her support and advice (and patience!) during the compilation of *Reflections*; to Felicity Ann Larard for drawing the main illustrations, including that on the front cover; to Creeds the Printers for their very helpful co-operation; to the many organisations which dealt so kindly with my enquiries; to the Dean and Chapter of Chester Cathedral for allowing me to use Henry Twells' poem, Time's Paces; to the staff of Dorchester branch of Dorset County Library, who were ever ready to guide me in my research; and last, but certainly not least, to all those readers of *Reflections* who so generously offered contributions for possible use in this revised second edition. To everyone, *Thank you*.

Maurice S. Ennals

West Stafford
Dorset

*I dedicate Reflections to
all those I love, especially
my wife Kay
and our children
Rosalyn,
David,
Patrick*

January

1 January – New Year's Day

A Happy New Year! What better time to recall those famous words of Minnie Louise Haskins, used by HM King George VI in his Christmas Day broadcast of 1939:

"I said to the man who stood at the Gate of the Year,
'Give me a light that I may tread safely into the unknown'.
And he replied, 'Go out into the darkness and put your
hand into the Hand of God. That shall be to you better
than light and safer than a known way'."

2 January

As we take our first fragile steps into another new year, the American writer, Ella Wheeler Wilcox (1850-1919), has this message for us in her poem The Winds of Fate:

One ship drives east and another drives west
With the selfsame winds that blow,
'Tis the set of the sails
And not the gales
Which tells us the way to go.

Like the winds of the sea are the ways of fate,
As we voyage along through life;
'Tis the set of a soul
That decides its goal,
And not the calm or the strife.

3 January

The New Year's Eve celebrations are over. The Christmas tree will soon be stripped of its decorations. The holly and mistletoe will be taken down. The greetings cards will be removed from the mantelpiece. The glad sounds of Christmas and New Year will become just memories. But there is no need for sadness. Spring will soon be here. The bulbs will be peeping through. The trees and hedgerows along our quaint Dorset lanes will be putting on their new coats of green. Marvellous, isn't it, the comings and goings of the seasons! Life is always full of new interests, new hope, new promise.

4 January

Here's love this New Year
To all those who I love,
And love to all those who love me;
Here's love to all those who love those who I love,
And to all those who love those who love me.

5 January

Twelfth Night! Years ago it was known as a night for revelry and various ceremonies. These days it is better known as the last night for taking down the decorations – otherwise bad luck will attend you! I still recall when, as a child, I saw my Mother and Father taking down the holly and tinsel. Then I'd work out how many more days till the next Christmas . . . only about 360! As we go through life we realise more and more that, eventually, all good things must come to an end. But, hopefully, there's always tomorrow, and the next day – and, surely, new joys will unfold.

6 January – Epiphany

When the wise men saw the star, they rejoiced with exceeding great joy. And when they were come into the house, they saw the young child with Mary his mother, and fell down, and worshipped him: and when they had opened their treasures, they presented unto him gifts; gold, and frankincense, and myrrh.

St. Matthew 2 : 10, 11.

7 January

Overheard in the garden . . . .

Said the Sparrow to the Robin,
"I would dearly like to know
Why these restless human beings
Rush about and worry so?"

Said the Robin to the Sparrow,
"I reckon that it must be
That they have no Loving Father
Such as cares for you and me."

8 January

It's amazing how little things stick in one's mind. Many years ago – more years than I care to remember! – I read these words in a friend's autograph book: 'If you want to help somebody to climb a hill you do not stand behind and push him; you go first and stretch out a helping hand'. It is the same with life, isn't it?

9 January

As in the wildest valley
You'll find a friendly breeze a-blowing,
So in the hardest heart
You'll find some tenderness a-showing.

10 January

It was on this day in 1989 that a dear relative, Keith, died suddenly at his home in the historic North Dorset town of Shaftesbury. A few months later his wife, Margaret, in her sorrow, penned some poignant words which I am privileged to use on this anniversary day:

> I dwelt in the desert of despair,
> It seemed I would live for ever there,
> Until one day my thornbush flamed with fire.
> He called to me, the God of my desire
> Right there among the thorn that tore my flesh;
> His glory shone. He said 'This ground is blessed.'
> My bush of thorns was not consumed, but glorified
> By one who knows what sorrow is, and died –
> Because He Cares.

11 January

After a particularly bad storm over Dorset in 1990 our road was alive with the sound of frenzied hammering as householders busily repaired fences that had been blown down. Why are we so fond of these barriers? Admittedly, they provide protection for children and animals, and make useful supports for chattering! But, in the United States neighbours live happily together without erecting barricades. Why, I wonder, can't we? After all, we're only too glad to open our gates to neighbours when we are in trouble.

12 January

It was almost a miracle that Jimmy reached his eighth birthday. He was badly burned in a serious road accident in Hampshire, in which his Mother was killed. In a burns unit near Salisbury a few days later, as he began to feel better, Jimmy said he was worried because it would soon be his birthday and, being in hospital, he was afraid no-one would send him any presents. That's where a BBC local radio station in Southampton came to the rescue. A listener explained the problem on the air. Within minutes, the station was inundated with telephone calls asking for Jimmy's full name and the hospital address. The result: Jimmy received over 500 cards, presents and gifts of cash. When we hear so much these days about selfishness and greed, isn't it nice to know there are still many thoughtful people in the world?

13 JANUARY

Verily I say unto you, Whosoever shall not receive the kingdom of God as a little child, he shall not enter therein. And he took them up in his arms, put his hands upon them, and blessed them.

St. Mark 10 : 15, 16.

14 JANUARY

Did you know that Winchester Cathedral has one of the most unusual statues to be found in any of our cathedrals? It is that of William Walker, a diver, who for some twenty years worked in the damp, marshy foundations into which the cathedral was sinking. Thanks largely to his labours, the cathedral was saved. I wonder how many of the thousands of people who visit this beautiful building each year, have ever heard of William Walker, or noticed his statue, let alone thanked God for his work?

15 January

Go bravely on doing the daily duties and trusting that as our day is so shall our strength be.

Edward King, Bishop of Lincoln 1885-1910.

16 January

Have you ever thought about the influence we have over other people in our daily lives? A thoughtless action or a careless word might easily cause distress to someone else – or a thoughtful action or an encouraging word might inspire another to follow your example. Don't let us think we are too unimportant, too insignificant, that others won't notice us. Every day our actions and words fall like pebbles in water, and their rippling circles of influence spread wider and wider over a much larger sphere than we realise.

17 January

For ten years I have known them as plain 'Mr. and Mrs. Smith'. For many more years they were known to variety theatre-goers as Renaldi and Karina – a dancing and acrobatic act. When they retired they opened a little Dorset tea-room – cream cakes an' all – at the village of Osmington, not far from Weymouth, and kept themselves busy in tea-room, kitchen and garden almost every waking hour. You may think, what's special about that? It's special because when in the autumn of 1995 they at last gave up serving their delightful teas and cakes, Mr. Smith was nearly ninety and Mrs. Smith nearly eighty – today is her birthday. They're a lovely couple, full of character – and what an example they set to those of us who are only too ready, come bus-pass time, to call it a day and bring out the bedroom-slippers.

18 January

Of all the gifts of life, When the toil of the day is o'er,
Give me a book and a fireside, I ask for nothing more.
However torn or tattered, However new or old,
A book to me at eventide, Is worth its weight in gold.
Not till my heart grows weary,
And my eyelids close in sleep,
Shall I forsake my silent friends, And leave in others' keep.

19 January

I don't know who it was who first said it, but it's so true '... The hardest arithmetic to master is that which enables us to count our blessings.'

20 January

Whatsoever things are true, Whatsoever things are honest, Whatsoever things are just, Whatsoever things are pure, Whatsoever things are lovely, Whatsoever things are of good report; If there be any virtue, And if there be any praise, Think on these things.

Philippians 4 : 8.

21 January

We'll call her Mrs. B. She lived in a Dorset village not far from Weymouth. When My Beloved called to see her she found Mrs. B. in one of her all-too-often bouts of depression. "If only I'd counted ten before saying it" ... "If only I'd thought before speaking" ... "If only, if only ... " So she went on.

"Don't upset yourself," My Beloved told her. "Not even our Heavenly Father can change the past." How right she was.

22 January

It was on this day in 1901 that the great Queen Victoria died. It might be worth recalling what she wrote in her diary on the day she ascended to the throne in 1837: "Since it had pleased providence to place me in this station I shall do my utmost to fulfil my duties towards my country. I am very young and perhaps in many, though not in all, things inexperienced, but I am sure that very few have more real goodwill and more real desire to do what is fit and right, than I have."

Victoria was then eighteen. For the next sixty-four years she showed that 'real goodwill' and 'real desire' to serve her country. What a majestic example she set – and what sound and solid foundations she laid for those who later wore the same crown.

23 January

Have mercy in victory, Courage in danger, Faith in the right; Love widely, Pray often, Be thankful, And do your duty at all times.

Wayfarer.

24 January

"Two single figures whom I saw from the carriage epitomised for me what Churchill meant to ordinary people: first, on the flat roof of a house, a man standing at attention in his old RAF uniform, saluting; and then, in a field some hundreds of yards away from the track, a farmer stopping work and standing, head bowed, cap in hand."

These were the words of one of Churchill's wartime secretaries, describing what he saw from the train carrying to a station near Blenheim Palace the body of Sir Winston, who died on this day in 1965. God grant that, when the time comes for us also to travel on, we too have earned the love and respect of our earthly fellows.

25 January

> God saw the road was getting rough,
> The hill was hard to climb,
> So he gently closed those weary eyes,
> And whispered 'Peace be thine'.

26 January

Do you collect autographs? I don't mean just signatures of well-known sportsmen and entertainers. I've got several books full of interesting sayings and little poems, written by loved ones and friends and people I have met over the years. I shall always have imprinted on my mind these words written by my dear Mother, who died on 26 January, 1954: 'A pessimist finds a difficulty in every opportunity; an optimist finds an opportunity in every difficulty.'

These words are just as true today as when they were written over fifty years ago.

27 January

Come unto me, all ye that labour and are heavy laden, and I will give you rest.

St. Matthew 11 : 28.

28 January

A prayer for today based on the words of Sir Francis Drake, who died at Portobello, in Panama, on this day in 1596: 'O Lord God, when thou givest to thy servants to endeavour any great matter, grant us also to know that it is not the beginning, but the continuing of the same, until it be thoroughly finished, which yieldeth the true glory.'

29 January

On her return from a short cruise, Kate told of the night a dense sea mist hung over the decks of the liner. "I was really afraid we might crash into another ship," she said, "but we kept on sailing through darkness. Afterwards I heard that, thanks to modern technology, the crew on the bridge could see ahead for a considerable distance. So I needn't have worried!"

Isn't it rather like that in life? So often we are fearful of the unknown. Dark and threatening clouds envelope us; and I don't believe – and I doubt if you do, dear reader – that every cloud has a silver lining. But I do believe, whatever our fears, He will always keep His promise: "I will not leave you comfortless".

30 January

Born on Monday, fair in the face;
Born on Tuesday, full of God's grace;
Born on Wednesday, sour and sad;
Born on Thursday, merry and glad;
Born on Friday, worthily given;
Born on Saturday, work hard for your living;
Born on Sunday, you will never know want.
19th century proverb.

31 January

A kind relative sent me the little card from Truro Cathedral. On it was printed the lovely 'story', Footprints … The story of a man who one night had a dream. He was walking along a beach with the Lord. Across the sky flashed scenes from his life. For each scene were two sets of footprints in the sand – one belonging to him, and the other to the Lord. After the last scene had flashed before him, he noticed that many times in his life there was only one set of footprints. This really bothered him, and he questioned the Lord about it. "Lord, you said that once I decided to follow you, you'd walk with me all the way, but I have noticed that during the most troublesome times in my life, there is only one set of footprints."

The Lord replied, "I love you and would never leave you. During your times of trial and suffering, when you see only one set of footprints, it was then that I carried you."

(Author unknown)

February

1 February

A prayer for this new month: 'Dear Father, I do not ask for skill or strength or power to achieve greatness. But I do ask Thee to help me to be loving and kind, to have patience towards my fellows, and to have understanding when their views differ from mine. Most of all, help me to remember that in quietness and in confidence we shall find our strength.'

2 February

If I remember rightly, Peter has been blind since birth. He was a working colleague in Southampton in the 1970's, and from the first day I met him I've never ceased to admire his zest for life, his wit and cheerfulness, and his determination to overcome the loss of a priceless gift so many of us take for granted. Peter is now a married family man, and has become one of the nation's best-known radio and television broadcasters.

What a wonderful example he sets – and what a wonderful example is set, too, by those dedicated volunteers who record, edit and supply what are known as Talking Newspapers for the Blind. The first 'Newspapers' in south-west Dorset were recorded in January 1988. Now, some 300 tapes – carrying local news, interesting topics, information, music, etc. – are distributed every week in, for example, Beaminster, Bridport, Dorchester, Portland,

Lyme Regis, Sherborne and Weymouth. God bless every volunteer and all those they serve.

3 FEBRUARY

Make the most of joy-filled days and thank God for them all.
Make the most of sunny hours before the shadows fall.
Make the most of what you learn with every passing year.
Do your best for those you love and help them while
they're here.

4 FEBRUARY

God is our refuge and strength, a very present help in trouble.   Psalms 46 : 1.

5 FEBRUARY

A little dog, the minister told his congregation, had no idea what was happening the other side of the door, or what it was like there – but he did know his master was there, and that was all that mattered. "And that," ended the minister, "is how we should view death. We know not what awaits us, but we do know that when we pass through the Door of Heaven we shall be with our Master – and that is all that matters. We must have in Him the same faith and trust that the little dog had in his master."

6 FEBRUARY

Worry is like a rocking-chair. It will give you something to do, but it won't get you anywhere.

7 FEBRUARY

He had no jewelled crown, He wore no diamond rings;
He owned no earthly throne. His name?
The King of Kings.

8 February

> I do dislike the winter dark,
> A creature of warmth am I;
> Yet winter's brown and gold
> Hold charm I can't deny.
> The all-embracing warmth of home
> Makes up for skies of grey,
> And hearts can look ahead
> To a brighter, sunny day.

9 February

If there's one thing I enjoy it is a long train journey. In spite of the reading I take with me, I seem to spend most of the journey 'sitting and staring' – watching the passing panorama of towns and villages, fields and farms. On one journey I passed through seven counties. With the 'cold' February sun shining, and plenty of room in the carriage, it was sheer delight! By the time I'd reached my destination I realised more than ever what beautiful countryside we are blessed with here in England. But God forbid that we should take it all for granted. Over the years green pastures and meadows and woods have disappeared to make way for development. Oh yes, of course we must have development, but eventually, surely, someone has got to say 'Enough is enough'. Otherwise, England will no longer be a green and pleasant land.

10 February

The Lord is my shepherd; I shall not want. He maketh me to lie down in green pastures; He leadeth me beside the still waters. Psalms 23 : 1, 2.

11 FEBRUARY

Going through some of my thousands of newspaper cuttings I came across an article about Mr. R. S., a village postman in Sussex. It told how he began his day at 5.35 a.m. sharp. After a quick cuppa, he jumped on his bicycle, and by 6.30 he was at the Post Office collecting his pile of letters and parcels. You may think there is nothing special about this. But, the article explained, apart from a break in the First World War, Mr. R. S. had been doing the job for sixty-eight years and had never once been late for work. His recipe for his long career? "Work." And for his happiness? "Staying busy."

What a tremendous example to those of us who tend to 'give up', and put up our feet, when we reach so-called retirement age.

12 FEBRUARY

Mind *when* you promise,
Mind *what* you promise,
Mind *where* you promise,
And mind you *keep* your promise.

13 FEBRUARY

Nobody sees the stranger come,
And nobody sees where he goes;
But he's always there when he's needed most,
A man whom nobody knows.
It happens a thousand times a day
Where tragedy, stark and grim,
Is thwarted by someone whom nobody knows.
I wonder – could it be Him?

14 February – St. Valentine's Day

A well-known encyclopedia recalled that 14 February was the day when birds were believed to begin mating. A happy thought, but does it really matter how observance of St. Valentine's Day started? What does matter is that each year on this day millions of people send greetings to a loved one. True love and true friendship are precious, indeed.

The fourteenth day of February,
Going on for Spring,
Declares the love I have for you –
That's why I wear your ring.

15 February

A friend and I were waiting for a bus near Lytchett Minster when my friend got in conversation with another man. For some reason they began talking about age, and the stranger said, "People can't believe I'm sixty-five. I look much younger. I hope you look as well when you reach my age."

"I hope I do," replied my friend.

Later, I asked my friend, "Why didn't you tell him you were seventy-one?" Came the reply, "That would have spoilt his day."

I learned at that moment a valuable lesson – always think before speaking.

16 February

> Friendship deep, true and real
> Is worthy of the name;
> Through sorrow, joy, despair,
> It'll always stay the same.

17 February

And now abideth faith, hope, charity, these three; but the greatest of these is charity.

1 Corinthians 13 : 13.

18 February

In our christian life I often think that some of us are rather like traffic lights – we keep going on and off. Some of us are like canoes – we need to be paddled along carefully. Some of us are like a car that won't start – we need a good push. Some of us are like a tennis ball – we don't know which way we'll bounce next. And some, thank goodness, are like the moon and the stars – bringing light where, otherwise, there would be darkness.

19 February

> Life is full of toil and trouble,
> Two things stand like stone:
> Kindness in another's trouble,
> Courage in our own.

20 February

Have you heard the famous tale of the ship which was beset in torrid heat off the South American coast? All the water casks were empty, and the crew were dying of thirst. Eventually, a rescue ship arrived, and sent the message 'Drop your buckets over the side and fill them . . . ' Unaware of their position, the crew of the beset ship did not realise they had drifted into the mighty estuary of the River Amazon – and all around them was fresh water, millions of gallons of it. Isn't there a lesson here for us? We, too, are afloat on a sea of plenty – a vast sea of daily blessings – yet often quite unaware of it, or, if we are aware, for some reason reluctant to acknowledge it.

21 February

It's about this time of the year that we observe Shrove Tuesday – the day before Lent begins, and the day for the increasingly-popular pancake races. The most famous, and oldest, pancake race of all is, of course, at Olney in Buckinghamshire. No-one, it seems, is quite certain how the Olney race originated, but, according to one story, a local housewife was making pancakes in the year 1445 when she heard the Parish Church shriving bell. Worried that she might be late for the service, she rushed out of the house complete with pan and cake! The traditional prize for the Olney winner has been a kiss from the verger! How good it is to see this ancient custom still part of our yearly calendar.

22 February

> A diamond in a rose bouquet
> Marked our joyful engagement day;
> Very soon, like the story of old,
> We both exchanged a band of gold.
>
> K. E. E.

23 February

For a friend and his wife in a small village in West Dorset it was one of those very special days – their Ruby Wedding. Everything went according to plan – a family gathering, lunch, toasts, photographs, etc. – until it came to cutting the cake at teatime. The happy couple noticed that two of their dearest weren't there. The explanation later was that they "Wanted to go to do a bit of shopping". I don't know how important the shopping was, but the celebrating couple were clearly a bit upset. Maybe we can all learn something from this little story. No matter how large the pond of happiness, it can still be disturbed by one tiny pebble of thoughtlessness.

24 February –

Anniversary of the start of the ground conflict in Kuwait, 1991

I am reminded today of a most touching poem I heard some years ago on the radio during a Remembrance Day programme . . .

What did you see, soldier? What did you see at war?
'I saw such glory and honour as I've never seen before.
'I saw men's hearts burned naked in red crucibles of pain,
 'I saw such Godlike courage as I'll never see again.'

What did you learn soldier? What did you learn at war?
'I learned that we must learn sometime what was not
learned before –
'That victories won on battlefields are victories
won in vain,
'Unless in peace we kill the germs that breed
new wars again.'

25 FEBRUARY

Greater love hath no man than this, that a man lay down his life for his friends.

St. John 15 : 13.

26 FEBRUARY

I always admired Mr. C. for his cheerfulness. No matter how difficult his problems – and he'd had plenty in his seventy-odd years – he always seemed to have a smile on his face . . . until that wet, cold morning in February when I ran into him in the shopping centre at Swanage. "Yes," he told me, "I've been up most of the night. My wife's not at all well. I think we've both got a bit rundown. But I suppose we ought to count our blessings. Things could be worse . . . " And then, suddenly, the customary, cheerful smile spread across his face.

Thank God for people like Mr. C. If we took the trouble to pause a moment and count our blessings, I reckon we'd be amazed how many we have. And a smile when the night is dark is worth twenty when the sun is shining.

27 FEBRUARY

Christ leads us through no darker rooms than He went through before.

28 February

"No need to thank me," said a friend at the end of our lane, after he had done me a little favour. "The pleasure was mine." And he meant what he said. He was one of those warm-hearted souls who really do find happiness in helping others – and in giving others pleasure. What a pity, isn't it, there are not more of his kind? If only we could all get into the habit of thinking of others before ourselves, what a different world it would be.

29 February – For Leap Year.

> Make the most of that extra day
> That February can bring:
> For now's the chance for you to ask
> Your Lochinvar for a ring!

March

1 March – St. David's Day

> Our Welsh friends have the greatest regard
> For the leeks that grow wild near Fishguard;
> And the echoes of drumbeats that boast
> Along the Pembrokeshire coast
> Beat out the message to say
> 'We'll celebrate on this National Day
> Our patron saint – St. David.'
>
> K. E. E.

2 March

I am the way, the truth, and the life: no man cometh unto the Father, but by me.

St. John 14 : 6.

3 March

An elderly gentleman who previously had been a regular attender at church, suddenly stopped going. The Vicar decided to visit him. He found Mr. M. at home, alone, sitting by the fire. The Vicar made himself comfortable in an armchair. After a few minutes he took the fire-tongs, picked up a brightly-burning ember and placed it to one side of the hearth. Very soon the flames of the lone ember died away; it became cold and grey. A few moments later the Vicar put the ember back in the fire. Immediately it began to glow again. The old gentleman looked across at his visitor. "Thank you," he said. "That was a marvellous, silent sermon. You will see me in my usual pew next Sunday." And he kept his promise. Come the next Sunday, he certainly was in his usual pew and – thanks to the Vicar's "silent sermon" – he continued to occupy it each week until his death.

4 March

They face force-nine gales, blizzards, thirty-feet waves, rain-storms, sub-zero temperatures. And they're all volunteers, except the full-time mechanic in each all-weather crew. Not difficult to guess who we're thinking of! Yes, it's the 3,500 men and women of the RNLI. Records show that as early as the 1770's attempts were made to provide a means of rescue to seafarers in distress. But it wasn't till this day – 4 March – in 1824 that the National Institution for the Preservation of Life from Shipwreck (as it was then called) was formed at a meeting in London.

Today, the RNLI – a registered charity – has 212 stations around the coasts of the UK and Ireland, manning nearly 300 boats; there are over 5,000 launches a year, and, since its founding on this day 172 years ago, more than 125,000 lives have been saved. These are just a few of the facts and figures about this fine organisation. Let's not forget them next time lifeboat flag-day comes round – nor the coastguards who work beside them on many a vital rescue.

5 March

There have been few more fateful days in our history than 5 March, 1936. It was at Eastleigh Airport, in Hampshire, that morning that the brilliantly-engineered Spitfire rose into the sky for the first time. Without for one moment forgetting the exploits of the famous Hurricane fighters, it was the Spitfire which caught a grateful nation's imagination – the 'plane that would for ever be the symbol of victory in the Battle of Britain.

With hearts apounding, And heads held high,
The Spitfire was scrambled, To win –
The triumph of the sky.

6 March

I don't know about you, dear reader, but epitaphs on gravestones and war memorials have long held a fascination for me. There's an unusual one in the now redundant church at Whitcombe, on the eastern edge of Dorset's county town of Dorchester. Repairs to the chapel floor in the 1970's uncovered this tender memorial to a baby by the name of Jejane Sherren, who died on 6 March 1815 at the age of '6 months one week and 5 days':

Grive not for me my Mother dear
But be content think unto you I was but lent
Short was my Days long is my Rest
God call'd me whenever he thought Best

7 March

It's about this time of the year that young hearts begin to think 'What can I give Mum for Mothering Sunday?' In the delightful Dorset village of West Stafford, where My Beloved and I have now lived for some years, we have enjoyed many a Mothering Sunday service at the little church of St. Andrew.

The festival was first celebrated in this country in the Middle Ages, when poor children worked as domestics and were usually allowed a day off to return home and take their parents gifts. In recent years Mothering Sunday has got more and more popular, and there's no mistaking the pleasure on those smiling faces as, walking down the aisle of their church, they present to Mum their gifts of a posy. Of all people who deserve a special day in the calendar it is Mothers the world over.

> Her love for you is deep and true,
> She'll help you see your troubles through;
> On Mothering Day you can enfold
> Her happiness with threads of gold.

8 March

M is for the million things she's given me;
O means to me she'll never grow old;
T is for the tears she's shed for me;
H is for her heart pure as gold;
E is for her eyes with love-light shining;
R means right, and right she'll always be.
Put them all together, Mother they spell –
The word that means everything – yes, everything – to me.

9 March

Know ye that the Lord he is God: it is he that hath made us, and not we ourselves; we are his people, and the sheep of his pasture . . . His mercy is everlasting: and his truth endureth to all generations.

Psalms 100 : 3, 5.

10 March

Have you still got that teddy-bear you treasured so much as a child? I wonder if you know how teddy-bears became so popular? In 1902, the then-President of the USA, Theodore Roosevelt, went on a bear-hunting trip (how could he be so cruel?), but one particular little bear cub 'touched the President's heart' and its life was saved. The incident caught the imagination of the public. An American shopkeeper began making toy bears to sell, and wrote to President Theodore – or, as he was popularly called, Teddy – to ask if he could use his 'nickname' for the new product. The President agreed, and soon the teddy-bear craze swept through the United States and eventually through Britain. Today, over ninety years on, teddy-bears are still very much part of our life and our families – thanks to an American President who spared the life of a wee cub in Mississippi.

11 March

Mrs. G. lived in a delightful house on the edge of the New Forest. But life for her had been far from delightful since the death of her husband. She was now clearly very lonely and 'down'. Chatting in her garden, she told me, "What is so disappointing, I have a married son and a married daughter within ten miles of here, and I hardly ever see them. They always seem to have some excuse. I know they have their own lives to live, but after all their Dad and I did for them when they were younger ... And when *my* Mum and Dad were alive I used to cycle regularly to see them, seven miles there and seven back. No car for me like the young people of today."

It wasn't difficult to understand how Mrs. G. felt. But I also had to remind her that not all young people are tarred with the same brush – thank goodness.

12 March

As children, My Beloved and I were taught by our parents to write thank-you letters for gifts received, and our children were taught the same. How times have changed. The children of today – even if they haven't the inclination or time (?) to write a letter – have only to lift the 'phone to say 'Thank you'. Oh, for the old-fashioned manners once drummed into us at home and at school – they stayed with us for life. Don't you agree?

13 March

The shadows dark would surely ne'er be seen,
Were there no sign of sunlight in between.

14 March

Cerne Abbas – with its Abbey remains, ancient church of St. Mary the Virgin, famous giant cut into the chalk hillside, and St. Augustine's Well – is undoubtedly one of Dorset's most sought-after villages. St. Augustine's Well is close by the graveyard, among lime trees and, according to legend, St. Augustine asked local shepherds whether they would prefer to have their thirsts quenched by water or beer. They chose the former, so St. Augustine struck the ground with his staff and, alas, appeared a small spring. Like all legends, you "accept it or forget it", as the saying goes. Either way, this one adds to the fascination of a lovely part of Dorset – and gives all of us something to talk about!

15 March

Blessed are they who understand my faltering step,
my shaking hand;
Blessed who know my ears today, are strained to catch
the things they say;
Blessed are all who seem to know, my eyes are dim,
my step is slow;
Blessed who with a cheerful smile, stop and
chat a little while.

16 March

Very, verily, I say unto you, He that heareth my word, and believeth on him that sent me, hath everlasting life, and shall not come into condemnation; but is passed from death unto life.

St. John 5 : 24.

17 March – St. Patrick's Day

St. Patrick used the shamrock to show by every leaf
The doctrine of the Trinity – the Emerald Isle's belief.
K. E. E.

18 March

The days are getting longer. The birds are beginning to sing. But even the seasons of Spring and Summer can't be all sunshine. Nor can our lives. There are times when we feel disappointed about the past, downcast about the present, and anxious about the future. It is at such times that I recall the inscription in a churchyard in Baltimore, USA:

'With all its shams, drudgery and broken dreams,
it is still a beautiful world.'

19 March

In 1979 Winchester Cathedral choir went on a concert tour of America. Returning home by air, the choir gave an unexpected piece of in-flight entertainment. At the request of a number of passengers, they sang Grace in Latin before a meal was served. As one of the passengers remarked later, it must have been the first time Grace had been sung in Latin over the Atlantic at 32,000 feet. What a memorable moment for everyone. Oh, for more such delightful memories.

20 March

We used to see his portrait on the back of the old £1 note – a book on his lap, and next to him a table with scientific instruments. In the bottom right corner of the note were the words: 'Sir Isaac Newton, 1642-1727'. Newton was born in the Lincolnshire village of Woolsthorpe. Sitting in his garden one day he saw an apple fall from a tree; this led him to the discovery of the law of gravitation. A devout Christian, Newton read The Good Book regularly. Viewing the greatness of God's world, he realised how little he really knew, and wrote, "I seem to have been like a boy playing on the seashore . . . now and then finding a smoother pebble or a prettier shell than ordinary, whilst the great ocean of truth lay undiscovered before me."

If Sir Isaac, who died on this day in 1727, could apply those words to *his* life, how much more relevant are they to ours?

21 MARCH

God send me a friend who may tell me of my faults; if not, an enemy, and he will.

17th century proverb.

22 MARCH

Sunday *is* different. And surely we should try to keep it that way. So often we don't appreciate something – until it is threatened.

Oh, blessed Sabbath, holiest of days,
We'll cling to thy sacredness for worship and praise!

23 MARCH

The Lord bless thee, and keep thee: The Lord make his face shine upon thee, and be gracious unto thee: The Lord lift up his countenance upon thee, and give thee peace.

Numbers 6 : 24, 25, 26.

24 March

On holiday in Cornwall a visitor from the lovely Dorset village of Owermoigne went to see the famous lighthouse that stands at the Lizard, the headland marking the most southerly point of Britain. With other holidaymakers, she was shown into the room that contains the equipment for operating the fog sirens. Then the group were taken up the stairs to have a look at the lantern – a beautiful piece of mechanism, and spotlessly clean. The lighthouse-keeper explained, "We polish the reflectors every morning."

The lady from Owermoigne told a friend later she had never forgotten that remark. "By our prayers each morning," she said, "we, too, can reflect light – the Light of the Holy Word, and shine as a light in what seems an ever-darkening world."

25 March

> We cannot change yesterday, that is clear,
> Or begin tomorrow, until it is here;
> So all that is left for you and for me
> Is to make today as sweet as can be.

26 March

I never did like hospitals. I doubt if many of us do. There was me, leg in plaster, and generally feeling rather despondent. Then I looked around . . . In the next bed was a World War II veteran still suffering from a shell wound after more than fifty years. In the bed opposite was an elderly gentleman who had broken both his legs. Outside in the corridor, a young fellow was being taken to the theatre for a serious operation. Suddenly, I realised how lucky I was. My problem could have been so much worse, and certainly I had no cause for self-pity. In that moment of reflection I learned a very real lesson. No matter how depressed, how despondent, we are, it's as certain as night follows day that there is someone else with a greater anxiety.

27 MARCH

> What love He showed upon the tree,
> What love, supreme, divine;
> What love He shows for me,
> What love He shows for mine.

28 MARCH

God give us the serenity to accept what cannot be changed;

Give us the courage to change what should be changed;
Give us the wisdom to distinguish one from the other.

Reinhold Niebuhr, 1892-1971.

(Attributed to, but not claimed by him.)

29 MARCH

Charles Wesley, England's greatest hymn-writer, died on this day in 1788. One of eighteen children (yes, eighteen), he spent many years travelling the country with his brother John, preaching, but in 1756 settled to home-life. He then spent most of his time preaching and writing hymns – 6,000 of them, according to early records. And the best loved of them? Very difficult to say, but certainly one that always uplifts me is 'Jesu, Lover of my soul'. How appropriate, as we remember Charles Wesley today, those last four lines in verse one:

> Hide me, O my Saviour, hide,
> Till the storm of life is past;
> Safe into the haven guide,
> O receive my soul at last.

30 MARCH

If you stand very still in the turmoil of life – And wait for the voice from within – You'll be led down the quiet ways of wisdom and peace – In a mad world of chaos and din ... If you stand very still and you hold to your faith – You will get all the help that you ask – You will draw from the silence the things that you need – Hope, courage, and strength for the task.

From 'Silence' by Patience Strong,
in her book Quiet Corner.

31 MARCH

Do all the good you can, By all the means you can,
To all the people you can, For as long as ever you can.

April

1 April – April Fools' Day

Apparently, there's no feasible explanation of the April Fool custom. As a little rhyme said in an almanac in 1760:

> The first of April some do say,
> Is set apart for All Fools' Day.
> But why the people call it so –
> Not I nor they themselves do know.

2 April

"Carpenter from Nazareth requires joiners. Apply within."
        Sign outside a church at St. Helen's, Merseyside.

3 April

I asked a friend who was convalescing after an illness how he was spending his time. "Oh, it's a bit of a problem," he replied. "Most of the day I watch television – that helps to pass the time." Helps to pass the time! I don't know about you, but time passes for me far too quickly. Even if I live to be 100 (which I doubt!), I'll never accomplish all the things I'd like to. And as we get older I'm sure we all regret the hours and opportunities we have wasted. As the oft-quoted words remind us (their authorship is much disputed): 'I expect to pass through this world but once.

Any good thing therefore that I can do, or any kindness that I can show to any fellow-creature, let me do it now; let me not defer or neglect it, for I shall not pass this way again.'

4 April

Loveliness needs not the foreign aid of ornament, but is when unadorned adorned the most.

5 April

I've still got the cutting. It is from the Sunday Express of 5 April 1987 – just five years to the day when the first ships of the British Task Force set sail for the South Atlantic, to fight and win the Battle of the Falklands: 'The men who fought and died and won so brilliantly . . . were there on behalf of the overwhelming majority of Britons who remembered the things this country stood for and who would not see its history or its traditions betrayed. On this anniversary of the day we began to recover our national pride, we remember and honour them all.'

6 April

Fear not, nor be dismayed, be strong and of good courage.
Joshua 10 : 25.

7 April

I wandered lonely as a cloud
That floats on high o'er vales and hills,
When all at once I saw a crowd,
A host, of golden daffodils,
Beside the lake, beneath the trees,
Fluttering and dancing in the breeze.

Yes, William Wordsworth, who was born in what is now known as the county of Cumbria on 7 April 1770. My Beloved and I spent a delightful holiday in Cumbria, and quickly came to realise how natural it was for Wordsworth and many other writers to be inspired by the beauty and tranquility of The Land of the Lakes. A farmer, tending his sheep near the fell village of Caldbeck, told us, "To fully appreciate the unrivalled scenery of the area it has to be seen under grey skies, even in storm, as well as in glorious sunshine." How right he was. Life's like that, too, isn't it? Very often the real strength and depth and loveliness of a person's character is seen at its best when skies are grey and the storms of life threaten.

8 April

The rung of a ladder was never meant to rest upon, but only to hold a man's foot long enough to enable him to put the other somewhat higher.

T. H. Huxley.

9 April

It was in, I think, our local evening newspaper, an item about the church clock at Sydling St. Nicholas, not far from Dorchester, chiming again – thanks to an anonymous donor who had kindly paid for it to be repaired. Nothing unusual about that, you'll say. But there is something unusual about the clock. It chimes the hours, but has no external face. Day after day it ticks away without any visible display or outward show. According to the church records it's probably the oldest clock of its kind in Britain. In a vague sort of way it reminds me of the many folk who, day after day, month after month, quietly get on with helping others without any outward show or parading of their thoughtful deeds. I call them the unseen – and often forgotten – Army of Good Samaritans.

10 April

> Some people just sit and wait for a chance –
> It isn't a wise thing to do;
> You've got to get up and get busy in search
> Of the chance that is waiting for you.

11 April

On Maundy Thursday, 11 April 1974, My Beloved and I attended Salisbury Cathedral for the distribution of the Royal Maundy by Her Majesty the Queen. This ceremony of great antiquity, which can be traced back with certainty to the twelfth century, derives its name from the Latin word 'mandatum', meaning a commandment, and after the processional hymn the opening words have always been 'A new commandment I give unto you . . . ' The choir sang the hymn 'Drop, drop, slow tears'. Perhaps you've sung it yourself at Eastertime, and can never fail to recall those last four lines:

> In your deep floods
> Drown all my faults and fears;
> Nor let His eye
> See sin, but through my tears.

12 April

And when they were come to the place, which is called Calvary, there they crucified him . . . Then said Jesus, Father, forgive them; for they know not what they do.

St. Luke 23 : 33, 34.

13 April

He came to earth that He might save . . . Then for His flock His blood He gave; Unafraid He heard them cry – 'Crucify him, Crucify'. A crown was placed upon His head . . . And to a cross the Christ was led; But the tomb held no power – Over God in that dark hour. Two days passed, then broke the dawn . . . Of the Resurrection Morn; Triumphant over death and pain, Jesus rose – And lived again!

14 April

Easter: the commemoration of Christ's rising, and the Spring festival when new life comes to earth after the long, dark Winter. The traditional symbols of Easter Day represent this new life: flowers, young animals, eggs. Many years ago in some countries, eggs were buried in the soil at planting time in the belief that they would bring life to new crops. Today, the newly-born animals and fragrant flowers continue to remind us of the miracle of Spring – and what would Easter Morn be without a gaily-wrapped egg?

15 April

God's love is knowing you need never walk alone.
Poster outside a Liverpool church after the Hillsborough football crowd disaster on 15 April, 1989.

16 April

When a new Manager was appointed to a football club in Wiltshire, one of the first things he did was to order smart blazers and ties for the players to wear on match days. "At first, there were the usual jokes," he said. "Someone suggested we looked like Glenn Miller's Band. But now my players are proud to wear them . . . " At the time I was associated with a club in Hampshire, and I still remember the Saturday when our opponents arrived, attired in their grey blazers and blue club-ties. "It's as good as a goal start for them," one of our players remarked. He was right! In the fourth minute of the game they scored. But, seriously, it's amazing what a difference it can make when one is dressed properly and smartly. I often wonder these days if our young people, in their jeans and track-suits, woollies and trainers, realise this.

17 April

> If your lips would guard from slips,
> Five things observe with care:
> Of whom you speak,
> To whom you speak,
> And how and when and where.

18 April

I'm sure most of us have heard of the hospital car service, provided by voluntary drivers for out-patients. After a patient had been supplied with transport, to take her to a hospital from her home in Wareham, she wrote a brief letter of thanks to the ambulance centre. "What a difference that letter made, especially to the volunteer driver," said a senior officer. "Every day we arrange journeys of this kind, but the thanks we get are so few." I believed him. A word of thanks doesn't take much effort – and certainly doesn't cost much! But it can mean such a lot. And, as the ambulance officer said, can make such a difference.

19 April

Today's date is one Burma veterans of the Second World War will never forget. It was on this day in 1944 that the Royal Berkshire Regiment raised the siege of Kohima, on the India-Burma border. For sixteen days the garrison of about 3,500 had held out against 15,000 Japanese, who laid down a murderous barrage from the heights around the town. The brave British and Indian troops – among them men of the 2nd Battalion, The Dorsetshire Regiment – stopped the Japanese march on Delhi. Here was seen some of the bloodiest fighting of all the Far East battles. Now, at Kohima, stands one of the most moving memorials of the war:

> When you go home
> Tell them of us and say
> 'For your tomorrow
> We gave our today'.

20 APRIL

It's a few years ago now, but I clearly recall asking the six-years-old son of a Christchurch friend what he would like to be when he grew up. Instantly, came the reply, "Not an engine-driver. I want to wear a helmet and be a policeman or a fireman".

Not for the first time, I thought about the tremendous debt we owe the men and women in the front-line of our emergency services. Almost daily they come face to face with disaster, danger, despair – and often death. I wonder how many of us pause, just occasionally for a couple of seconds, to say a silent "Thank you"?

> Be England what she will,
> With all her faults she is my country still,
> And those who shirk to serve I count for nil.

21 APRIL

I wonder if you've heard of Dorton House School at Sevenoaks, in Kent? It's a school for blind children, run by the Royal London Society for the Blind. I had the privilege of visiting Dorton House. What wonderful work I saw being done there – and what bonnie children, trying so bravely to overcome their terrible handicap. Many of those I met faced a lifetime of blindness. But they were so cheerful and so determined to do well in their studies and sports activities – a marvellous example to all of us who are blessed with the precious gift of sight. And take it so much for granted.

22 April

> I go to the seaside every year.
> I swim in the sea without any fear.
> I run, and shout, and dance with glee.
> There isn't a girl as happy as me.
> I paddle, and jump over the billowing waves.
> I dig deep in the sand, and make unfilled graves.
> I search till I find a beautiful shell,
> And, at the end of the day, all is well.

This was a verse written by one of the blind students at RLSB's Dorton House. The title: 'A Child's Happiness'. It was composed by Clare Page, then aged ten, and note that last line: 'And, at the end of the day, all is well'. Makes you wonder, doesn't it, why we are so ready to complain and grumble when all is not well . . .

23 April – St. George's Day

The anniversary of the tragic death of the popular young English poet, Rupert Brooke. He was only in his twenty-eighth year when he died of blood poisoning in the Greek island of Skyros, in 1915. Who can ever forget possibly the best known of his poems, 'If I should die . . .' written when he was a naval officer in training at Blandford? I recall some words of it here, providing as it does his own sad epitaph:

> If I should die, think only this of me:
> That there's some corner of a foreign field
> That is for ever England. There shall be
> In that rich earth a richer dust concealed;
> A dust whom England bore, shaped, made aware,
> Gave, once, her flowers to love, her ways to roam,
> A body of England's, breathing English air,
> Washed by the rivers, blest by suns of home.

24 April

Memorials to past heroism are a timely reminder of the need for vigilance in the future.

25 April – Anzac Day

First World War veterans remember with pride the anniversary today of the first landings at Gallipoli in 1915. A quarter-of-a-million Allied troops – British, Australian, New Zealand, French – were involved. In the next eight-and-a-half months more than 100,000 lives were lost in fighting as bloody and strategically-inconclusive as any in the war.

'Their name liveth for evermore.'

26 April

Oft' times we take for granted all the kindliness of people near and dear to us. By deed, word or caress we can show we know and notice and appreciate.
There's nothing half so sad as to remember this . . . too late.

27 April

Peace I leave with you, my peace I give unto you: not as the world giveth, give I unto you. Let not your heart be troubled, neither let it be afraid.

St. John 14 : 27.

28 April

The only thing necessary for the triumph of evil is for good men to do nothing.

Edmund Burke.

29 April

They've brought you up to date, Lord, at the church where I go . . .
They've written brand-new hymns with tunes that I don't know,
So I hardly ever sing now, though I did love singing so.
They've modernised the Bible, the Lord's Prayer and the Creed,
When the old ones were so perfect that they filled my every need.
It can't be very long now before I'm called above,
And I know I'll find you there, Lord, and glory in your love.
So till then I'll stick it out here, though it's not the same for me,
But while others call you 'you', Lord, do you mind if I say 'Thee'?

30 April

Mrs. E. said she was at her "wits' end" (whatever that means!). Her young grand-daughter's birthday was at the end of May, and the trouble was – she told me as we chatted in her garden – "She's got just about everything she could wish for. Bicycle, clothes, skates, books, doll's pram, and dolls and teddies galore. Part of the trouble," she went on, "is all the advertisements for kids' things on TV. It must be hard for Mums and Dads who can't afford every time to say 'Yes, alright'. I shall never forget how hard I had to save up for my first bike. I know that made me appreciate it more and look after it."
Mrs. E. certainly had a fair point. So often the more we have in life, the more we want, and the more we get what we want the more, sadly, we take it all for granted.

May

1 May

Maybe it's a sign of the times in which we live, but I think it sad that we don't observe May Day as we used to. This was the day on which we celebrated the end of the drab winter months – and the blooming of the new, Spring flowers. Young and old danced round the decorated maypole, which was supposed to symbolize the fresh life pushing up from under the soil. In a few places we can still see maypole dancing – and certainly in Dorset, Morris dancing – but over recent years the first day of May has been set aside for workers' parades and demonstrations, especially in mainland Europe. As an elderly neighbour said to me, "How much more romantic it was to see the children in their pretty clothes dancing round the pole." You can say that again!

2 May

The scene's ablaze with splendour . . . Nature's wonders live again – Bathed in brilliant sunshine . . . Freshened by gentle rain. Overhead a sky so blue . . . Fields of lambs and rip'ning corn – Everywhere new, young life . . . Faith, hope and strength reborn. Now heavy hearts are lightened . . . Dark wintery days have passed – Another gift from God . . . For Spring is here – at last!

3 May

Love knows no divisions, but adds and multiplies as we share it with others.

4 May

Thou shalt love the Lord thy God with all thy heart, and with all thy soul, and with all thy mind, and with all thy strength: this is the first commandment. And the second is like, namely this, Thou shalt love thy neighbour as thyself. There is none other commandment greater than these.

St. Mark 12 : 30, 31.

5 May

> Look always on the sunny side,
> 'Twill make us happier far;
> Why should we try to find the cloud
> When brightly shines the star?

6 May

My Beloved and I were visiting a little church in North Dorset when we noticed on a table by the door some small cards bearing the famous prayer of St. Francis of Assisi. The son of a wealthy merchant, Francis took a life of poverty, spending his time preaching, and eventually founded the Franciscan Order. For today's reflection, I pass on to you part of his prayer:

Lord, make me an instrument of your peace.
Where there is hatred, let me sow love; Where there is injury, pardon; Where there is discord, union; Where there

is doubt, faith; Where there is despair, hope; Where there is darkness, light; Where there is sadness, joy . . . It is in giving that one receives, It is in pardoning that one is pardoned, And it is in dying that one finds Eternal Life.

7 May

A young lad was sitting in a hospital waiting-room, about to be admitted for an operation. After a few minutes a nurse came in, and called out "Paul Jones". Immediately the lad, with a broad smile on his face, enquired, "This, I presume, nurse, is instead of the last waltz?" What a blessing it is to have a sense of humour at a time of adversity!

8 May

'Blessing of animals' services have become increasingly popular in recent years. The younger members of churches certainly seem to enjoy them – possibly more than the animals do! It was Rogation Sunday, 8 May in 1994, that My Beloved and I went to such a service in Dorset at the little Methodist Chapel at Broadmayne. The Minister, the Reverend Barrie Snook, from the United Church at Dorchester, welcomed each animal by name – Smokey and Lucky, Ben and Trigger, Fluffy and Sniffles and Fruffy (they're the ones I remember!), and went on to remind us of the important part pets play in our daily lives. This is especially true, isn't it, as the years go by, and a feeling of possible loneliness begins to occupy our thoughts. As an elderly widow said, stroking the tabby on her lap, "I don't know what I'd do without Blackie – I really don't . . . "

9 May

John didn't think much of the new Deputy Headmaster at his school; in fact, for some reason he took a considerable dislike to him. In the four weeks since Mr. E. had joined the staff he had disciplined John three times. "Any more trouble with you," said Mr. E., "and I shall report you to the Head . . . " Two weeks later John was taken ill – just as he was preparing for examinations. He needn't have worried. Two evenings a week for the next five weeks Mr. E. went to John's home and helped him with his studies. Fortunately, John was fit enough to return to school in time for the examinations. He gained four 'passes'. And the first person he thanked when he got the results? Mr. E., of course.

Just shows, doesn't it, that we should not be too hasty in our judgement of other people.

10 May

I can see it now, the little brown frame and the poem it contained. Who wrote the words I could never find out, but I did find them comforting after a particularly trying day.

Sleep sweetly in this quiet room,
O thou, whoe'er thou art;
And let no mournful day now passed,
Disturb thy peaceful heart.
Forget thyself and all the world, Put out each garish light;
The stars are shining overhead, Sleep sweetly then,
GOODNIGHT!

11 May

Heaven and earth shall pass away, but my words shall not pass away. St. Matthew 24 : 35.

12 May

> If you don't like life, it's the way you're livin',
> A little less takin', a bit more givin',
> A little less hatin', a little more lovin',
> A little less shovin', a little more helpin',
> A little more smilin', and not so much strife,
> And soon you'll be in love with life.

13 May

> It was Monday morning in the village of Portesham. A boy of about nine was waiting to cross the road while clutching the hand of his young sister. He looked this way and that, and was uncertain. Then a man, umbrella in hand, came along and shepherded the children across the road. Immediately the boy took off his school-cap and smiling, said, "Thank you, sir." The man saluted him – "My pleasure," he said.
>
> This delightful incident made a friend's day. How true it is that a simple, apparently insignificant little happening of this kind can mean such a lot. There is so much happiness in life if we would only look for it – and try to give it.

14 May

> O Lord, I pray, help me with my tasks this day,
> And at the end may I kneel and say, "Thank you".

15 May

> I've often had to go without the things money can buy, but thankfully I've had most of the things money cannot buy.
>
> Lester Melbray

16 (and 17) May

'Perhaps the greatest single feat of arms in World War Two' – that's how the breaching of the Mohne and Eder dams in Germany by Lancasters of 617 Squadron has been described. The anniversary of the raid by the famous Dam Busters in 1943 falls today. Dorset has a special reason to remember it, because it was on the waters of the Fleet by Chesil Beach that Barnes Wallis tested the prototypes of the 'bouncing' bombs. The raid meant the sacrifices of many lives. Of the nineteen 'planes that set out from RAF Scampton, only eleven returned; fifty-six men out of 133 were lost, three of them escaping death by parachute to spend the rest of the war as prisoners. How appropriate and deserving those words of Marshal of the RAF Lord Tedder:

"Here was leadership which inspired men to face up to, and overcome, 'impossibilities'. May their example be an inspiration to us now and in the future."

17 May

They that wait upon the Lord shall renew their strength; they shall mount up with wings as eagles; they shall run, and not be weary; and they shall walk, and not faint.

Isaiah 40 : 31.

18 May

There's a Flower of Memory in the Garden of Life
That changes as time passes by;
New petals are born, some petals fade,
But few seem ever to die.
They vary in colour, in size and in shape,
And some keep their freshness for years;
Some give pleasure and joy to us all,

While others bring sadness and tears.
There's one thing I know of this wondrous bloom,
All of its petals are ours,
And we'd be the poorer if the Garden of Life
Had not Memory as one of the flowers.

19 May

It was on this day in 1935 that the legendary Lawrence of Arabia died at Bovington Camp in Dorset, after a motorcycle accident six days earlier near Moreton. Lawrence is buried at Moreton, and annually after his death – until 1994 – an unknown admirer in America arranged to have placed on his grave on the date of his birthday, 16 August, a bunch of white roses, with one bloom fewer each year. Fifty years after Lawrence's death – on 19 May, 1985 – a special service was held at the village church of St. Nicholas. At the time of the service a note appeared on his grave: 'You will never be forgotten. May your soul rest in peace'. Appropriate, indeed. Lawrence's name will certainly live long in the history of this land, and it was in Dorset, especially at his tiny cottage at Clouds Hill, that he sought the peace and obscurity that had eluded him in his turbulent life. At Bovington Tank Museum there is a superb exhibition to his memory.

20 May

Nothing is so hard for those who abound in riches as to conceive how others can be in want.

Jonathan Swift.

21 May

Asked by the teacher what she thought her Mother would like for her birthday tomorrow, the little girl replied, "I know Daddy would like to give her a new dress, my brother would like to give her a purse, and Mummy would like a day off."

Out of the mouth of babes . . .!

22 May

> I sought my soul, but my soul I could not see;
> I sought my God, but my God eluded me;
> I sought my brother – and I found all three.

23 May

When next you cross the Dorset border into Devon, it's not many miles to the delightfully-named town of Ottery St. Mary. It was here that Samuel Taylor Coleridge was born in 1772. He was the son of the Vicar of St. Mary's, and in the church there's a memorial tablet to Coleridge. It bears words from his famous poem, The Ancient Mariner: 'He prayeth best who loveth best'. Need any more be said?

24 May

> Twilight and evening bell.
> And after that the dark!
> And may there be no sadness of farewell,
> When I embark.
>
> Alfred, Lord Tennyson

25 May

> Links of steel may rust and sever,
> True friendship links last for ever.

26 May

Who could ever forget this fateful day of 1940? Certainly not those of us old enough to remember. It was on 26 May that the evacuation of Allied Forces from Dunkirk began. Over the next nine days more than 330,000 servicemen were rescued – thanks to the bravery of those manning the big and little ships, and the valour of another 3,000 men who fought the last rearguard action. I recall the famous lines written by C. Day-Lewis:

> Soldiers on a foreign shore
> In sight of home we fought, we died.
> The flames of Calais flashed our last
> Message across the sundering tide –
> Tell them at home their English lads
> Fought well, sleep well, side by side.

27 May

And God shall wipe away all tears from their eyes; and there shall be no more death, neither sorrow, nor crying, neither shall there be any more pain: for the former things are passed away.

Revelation 21 : 4

28 May

I pass on to you a little Christian Aid Week story I heard a few years ago. A hungry young girl in a city slum in South America prayed very hard for some food and toys, but nothing happened. She told this to a cynical friend who said, "What happened to this God of yours? Why didn't he answer your prayers?" Replied the young girl: "Oh, I'm sure he did. He asked someone to bring me the food, but whoever it was must have forgotten."

29 May

Loved ones come into our lives . . .
> We kiss, they give a loving smile
> And loving, walk with us a mile,
> Then, for reasons unbeknown,
> Only stay a while.
> They pass beyond our reach,
> Not even a fond 'Good-bye';
> I do not understand.
> Maybe God knows why.

30 May

> We are writing a gospel, a chapter each day
> On all that we do and on all that we say;
> People read what we write, whether false or true,
> Pray, what is the Gospel according to You?

31 May

The little cares that fretted me, I lost them yesterday
Among the fields above the sea, Among the winds at play,
Among the lowing of the herds, The rustling of the trees,
Among the singing of the birds, The humming of the bees.

The foolish fears of what might pass, I cast them all away
Among the clover-scented grass, Among the new-mown hay,
Among the rustling of the corn, Where ill-thoughts die and good are born
– Out in the fields with God.

> Poem read at
> Service of Thanksgiving
> for the life of a 92-year-old lady,
> at St. Peter's Church, Shaftesbury, on this day in 1996.
> The author is unknown.

June

1 June

I am the good shepherd: the good shepherd giveth his life for the sheep.

St. John 10 : 11.

2 June

The anniversary of the coronation of Her Majesty Queen Elizabeth the Second in 1953. In the evening, after all the ceremonial, she made what will go down in history as one of her most moving broadcasts to the Commonwealth. Those of us old enough to remember, may recall these words: "I have in sincerity pledged myself to your service, as so many of you are pledged to mine. Throughout all my life, and with all my heart, I shall strive to be worthy of your trust."
The pledge she has certainly kept, and our trust in her has surely never, never been in doubt.

3 June

Yesterday, the second day of June, is a date surely all good people of Dorset should be able to associate with possibly the county's most famous son. But I wonder how many of us can? Yes, Thomas Hardy was born – in 1840, in a cottage in the village of Higher Bockhampton, near Dorchester. In 1926 Hardy celebrated his eighty-sixth birthday by writing 'He Never Expected Much'. In his book about Hardy's 'Life and Work', F. H. Halliday recalls that T. H. has a chat with the world:

> Well, World, you have kept faith with me,
> Kept faith with me;
> Upon the whole you have proved to be
> Much as you said you were.
> Since as a child I used to lie
> Upon the leaze and watch the sky,
> Never, I own, expected I
> That life would be all fair.

4 JUNE

The Allies finally surrendered at Dunkirk. The last men were evacuated. As it's often said, when the night seems at its darkest, so follows quickly the breaking of dawn. And it was on this day in 1940 that Winston Churchill told the world:

"We shall defend our island, whatever the cost may be, we shall fight on the beaches, we shall fight on the landing-grounds, we shall fight in the fields and in the streets, we shall fight in the hills; we shall never surrender."

5 JUNE

Simon wasn't his usual self. "What's worrying you?" I asked him. "I'm furious with myself," he replied. "I promised to meet an old pal at the club a couple of nights ago, but I'd had a busy day, I was tired, and it was late. So I 'phoned the club and left a message saying that, after all, I couldn't meet him. But it didn't end there . . . This morning I had a message from John's wife. He'd suddenly been taken ill and was in hospital. That's taught me a lesson, that has. From now on, I'll do my damndest to keep any promise I make – and, whenever possible, not put off till tomorrow what ought to be done today."

6 JUNE – D-Day

Thursday, 6 June, 1944. D-Day. General Eisenhower had said "Let's go." Operation Overlord was underway – an operation which had taken three years to plan. Over 150,000 Allied servicemen began landing in France by air and sea – among them men of the Devonshire, Dorsetshire and Hampshire Regiments (as they were then known). Poole, Portland and Weymouth were major embarkation ports. During the night, gliders carrying men of the 6th Airborne Division, had been towed to Normandy from RAF Tarrant Rushton, between Wimborne and Blandford. Their task: to capture vital territory, including the famous Pegasus Bridge. Within the next twenty-four hours 10,000 men – mainly British, Canadian and American – had been killed or wounded or were missing.

We forget at our peril the sacrifices of that night and day, and the days to follow. Any nation which betrays such heroes disregards its noble past and undermines its future.

7 JUNE

And he shewed me a pure river of water of life, clear as crystal . . . And there shall be no night there; and they need no candle, neither light of the sun; for the Lord God giveth them light: and they shall reign for ever and ever. Revelation 22 : 1, 5.

8 June

No wonder each year thousands of visitors to Dorset head for Furzebrook, near Wareham . . . to view one of the county's leading tourist attractions, the Blue Pool. The pool was cut into the landscape by clay-diggers in the 19th century, and the diffraction of light from minute particles of clay suspended in the water creates an illusion of colour from deep blue to shades of green, depending, I'm told, on the variations of cloud and sun. The pool was first opened on this day in 1935. Many people who go there regularly are convinced that the water appears to be a different colour every day. "One day one colour, one day another!" said a friend. I cannot vouch for that, but I clearly recall a remark my friend made after one of his visits, "Our life day by day is like that, isn't it? One day full of colour and promise, and the next . . . well, you know what I mean." I certainly do.

9 June

Young Jimmie got into a habit he found it difficult to get out of. Every night without fail, after he had been in bed for about half-an-hour, he would go to the top of the stairs and shout, "Mum! Dad! Is there anyone there?" After he had been assured there was, he got back into bed and so off to sleep. It was just that comforting assurance he wanted. And it's the same with most of us, isn't it? As long as we know there is someone else around, a Good Samaritan on the same road, someone to share our problems with. It makes such a difference.

10 June

Many years ago I knew and loved a very brave little girl. Her name was Mary, and she lived in Middlesex. While still a school-girl she contracted cancer in a leg. In spite of all the efforts of hospital staff, Mary eventually had to have the leg amputated. But she still kept cheerful, and set a wonderful example to all of us. How thrilled she was, and how proud, when – as a reward for her cheerfulness and bravery – she was presented with the Girl Guides' 'VC'. Not long afterwards Mary died, on 10 June, 1945, aged thirteen. Looking through one of my autograph books I found these four lines she had written a few years earlier:

> Little deeds of kindness,
> Little deeds of love,
> Make this world an Eden –
> Like the Heaven above.

11 June

Suffer the little children to come unto me, and forbid them not: for of such is the kingdom of God.

St. Mark 10 : 14

12 June

I wonder what the name Augustus Toplady means to you? About the year 1762, when he was an Anglican curate in Somerset, he was walking in the Mendip Hills and suddenly there was a severe storm. He found shelter in the cleft of a large rock. As he waited there for the rain and thunder to abate, he thought how God protected him, like the rock was protecting him, and he began to write one of our best-loved hymns, 'Rock of ages, cleft for me, Let me hide myself in Thee'. I'm told you can still see the rock in Burrington Cove and read, carved on it, 'Rock of Ages'. The lovely hymn means more to me each time I sing it; You, too, I'm sure . . . especially the third verse:

> Nothing in my hand I bring,
> Simply to thy Cross I cling;

> Naked, come to thee for dress;
> Helpless, look to thee for grace;
> Foul, I to the fountain fly;
> Wash me, Saviour, or I die.

13 June

The patient, a middle-aged businessman, had been in hospital several weeks, had two operations, and – in the words of a friend – "Had received wonderful care from the nursing staff". When the day came for his discharge he hardly said a word of thanks. How different was the appreciation of an old lady who went into the same hospital for less than a week. Only an hour after her discharge a bouquet of flowers arrived, addressed to the doctors and nurses. Attached was a simple card, 'With my thanks for all your kindness.' As one of the nurses said, "It was only a small bouquet, but it was the thought that mattered."

14 June

> God takes us one by one
> And breaks the family chain;
> But somewhere in a better land
> Our chain will link again.
> Your memory is a keepsake,
> With which we'll never part;
> God keep you in His arms
> As He heals our broken hearts.

15 June

When we think we know best and get all wrapped up in ourselves, we make a pretty small package.

16 June

> True friends are like diamonds,
> Precious and rare;
> False friends are like Autumn leaves,
> Found everywhere.

17 June

Life's field will yield as you sow it, a harvest of flowers or thorns.

18 June

A neighbour, during a visit to Parkstone, was suddenly surrounded by a small crowd of so-called football supporters – hooligans, I prefer to call them. They were shouting and waving rattles and scarves, and the elderly lady found herself with other shoppers almost pushed off the pavement. Then, further along the street she noticed a young airman, immaculate in his blue uniform, helping a blind lady and her guide-dog across the road. "There's hope yet for the younger people, isn't there?" my neighbour said that evening. She was right. But was it more than a coincidence that the young man she was obviously talking about was in uniform?

19 June

Forgive and forget, we're told. The trouble is, some people are never for giving and others are always for getting.

20 June

I wonder if you've noticed how sometimes a small happening in our lives – something seemingly quite insignificant at the time – can turn out to be one of considerable importance and meaning? I remember the story of the businessman who told his friends, "That first meeting with Jean at a party near Beaminster was the most wonderful thing that ever happened to me."

"David," replied one of his friends, "that's nonsense. I was at that party. You hardly spoke to her." David disagreed. And he was right. It may not have appeared so that evening, but that first meeting led to a second meeting, then a third . . . and eventually to the altar.

The world must be littered with tales of this kind: a chance meeting, a handshake, a kiss, a journey, a letter. There's a saying about great oaks growing from little acorns. It carries a lot of truth.

21 June

Today is the harvest of yesterday, and the seedtime of tomorrow.

22 June

Jesus Christ the same yesterday, and today, and for ever.
Hebrews 13 : 8

23 June

> My will is not my own
> Till thou hast made it thine;
> If it would reach a monarch's throne
> It must its crown resign.
> George Matheson (1842-1906)
> *(From 'Make me a captive, Lord'.)*

24 June

Though 'Farewell' I had to say – Back in the distant past, My memories of you Home-town – Are memories that will last. My thoughts are always with you – And these shall remain . . . Until my task is o'er – And I come home again.

I miss my friends and dear ones – Their kind, smiling faces; I miss my favourite haunts – And other going-places. Yes, I miss you dear home-town – And when my work is through . . . I promise I'll return – To live-out my days with you.

25 June

Did you know that The Good Book has now been translated, in full, in 300 languages? Parts of it have been translated into another 800 languages, and the whole of the Gospel of St. Luke is now available in 900 languages. If for the rest of your life you could have only one book or gospel to read, I wonder which you would choose? Before deciding I would have to think that over very, very carefully. You, too, I guess!

26 June

If you're interested in places of pilgrimage, don't overlook one of Hampshire's best-known villages – Selborne, a few miles south of Alton. This is where the famous naturalist-parson, the Reverend Gilbert White, was born in 1720, and in the Parish Church of St. Mary there is a memorial stained-glass window. White's house is now a museum. Here is his library, together with mementoes of Captain Lawrence Oates, the explorer who accompanied Scott to the South Pole, walking to his death in a blizzard. Oates had no links with Selborne, but a member of the family, seeking a suitable place to house family memorabilia, bought White's house and set up a trust fund to administer a combined Oates and White museum.

Gilbert White is buried in the churchyard, his gravestone marked 'G.W. 26 June 1793'. Lawrence Oates' body was never found, but a cairn, placed near to where he gave his life, described him as 'A very gallant gentleman'. Two simple inscriptions. Yet who could forget them? So often in life it is the simple things, the simple words, the simple actions, we remember most.

27 June

I shall never forget the story told me by a community nurse – one of those kind and caring people who tend to the sick in their own homes. On a visit to a patient in a village near Bridport, she found the elderly lady watching on television the funeral of Pope John. "I don't hold with this religious stuff," said the patient, "but him, he were a lovely fella."

"What eulogy could beat those few words?" remarked the nurse, recalling her visit to the elderly lady. Her question required no answer. We don't have to be a fluent after-dinner speaker to explain our feelings or thoughts. The most telling are often the briefest.

28 June

Who shall separate us from the love of Christ? Shall tribulation, or distress, or persecution, or famine, or nakedness, or peril, or sword? Nay, in all these things we are more than conquerors through him that loved us.

Romans 8 : 35, 37.

29 June

God gave all men all earth to love,
But, since our hearts are small,
Ordained for each one spot should prove
Beloved over all.

Rudyard Kipling

30 June

I read in a Dorset magazine about the wee laddie who was asked if he said his prayers every night. "No," came the reply. "Mum says them for me. She says, 'Thank God you're in bed at last'." Amazing, isn't it, what Mums do for their children!

July

1 July

From Sherborne to Cerne – from Horton to Bill –
From Tolpuddle, Wimborne and Corfe Castle Hill –
From Wareham to Bridport, Lydlinch and Came,
See the beauty of Dorset – the County of Fame!

Kay Ennals.

2 July

Lord, help me today to make my words tender and sweet; tomorrow I may have to eat them.

Lester Melbray

3 July

I read the story in a local newspaper. It told how, apart from the war years, Bert of Lyme Regis had been caring for the Parish Church clock since 1936. This meant climbing the tower twice a week to wind the wheels of the over one-hundred-years-old clock. Now, at seventy-one, Bert was hanging up the key. Just think of the many thousands of steps he had climbed in half-a-century! As the Vicar said, "Local residents and visitors alike have depended on this clock." They'd depended even more on Bert. So often in life we take familiar things for granted, forgetting the effort and thought that often have to go into them.

4 July

It's some years ago now, but I well recall the occasion when a friend living at Wimborne Minster put one of the old £1 notes in an envelope with a birthday card and gave it to his five-year-old niece. Opening the envelope, she took out the note and gave it back to her uncle. "Thank you very much, Uncle," she said. "But I can't be greedy – I've already got one of these."

I reckon in that little story there's a hidden message for some of us older ones, don't you?

5 July

Life is full of opportunities to go the extra mile,
Of bringing sunshine to a face
That has somehow lost its smile;
Life is full of opportunities to help see people through,
And if you do your best for them,
They'll do their best for you.

6 July

We all have our memories – Thoughts that will never die . . . Thoughts of the olden times – Times now gone by; As every new dawn breaks, So grows that precious store – Of things that happened in the past . . . In days gone before. So many, many memories – Some happy ones, some sad . . . Some that cause me sorrow – Some that make me glad; But each a treasure on its own – That from me will never part . . . Those memories always lingering there – In the bottom of my heart.

7 July

Blessed is the man that endureth temptation: for when he is tried, he shall receive the crown of life, which the Lord hath promised to them that love him.

James 1 : 12.

8 July

I still smile when I recall the tale of the little girl who was given by her Dad twenty-pence to put in a charity collection-box. Later, her Mother casually asked her, "You did put in the box all the money your Father gave you?" Jane hesitated. "Not quite all of it, Mum," she replied. "You see, at Sunday School teacher told us that Jesus loves a cheerful giver. Well, I knew I'd be more cheerful if I gave ten-pence and kept ten-pence for myself."
Ah well, we were all young once!

9 July

He never won the Derby or the Grand National, yet he was probably the best known horse in the country. Yes, Sefton, the heroic Household Cavalry veteran. Old age did what the IRA failed to do in the horrific Hyde Park bombing of 1982. On 9 July 1993 animal lovers were saddened by the news that, after going incurably lame, Sefton had been put down at the age of thirty at a military veterinary centre in Melton Mowbray. Newspapers searched for an appropriate epitaph. I prefer the words specially written for the Horse of the Year Show by Ronald Duncan nearly forty years ago:

'Where in this wide world can man find nobility without pride, friendship without envy, or beauty without vanity? Where grace is laced with muscle, and strength by gentleness confined. He serves without servility; he has fought without enmity . . . England's past has been borne on his back. All our history is his industry. We are his heirs, he our inheritance. Ladies and Gentlemen – the Horse!'

10 July

It was 10 July, 1990 – fifty years to the day since the officially-recognised start of the Battle of Britain (what has been described as the 'main phase' began on 8 August). A lone ex-airman, service cap in hand, stood silently by an RAF memorial at Crossways, four miles outside Dorchester. The memorial – five-feet high, roughly hewn out of local stone – was erected by members of the Royal Air Forces Association to mark the site of the now-closed RAF Warmwell airfield during the Second World War. The memorial recalls 'those men and women who whilst serving with the Royal Air Force, United States Army Air Force, Military and Allied Forces at RAF Warmwell, made the Supreme Sacrifice in defence of freedom. Lest we forget.'

I wonder what memories passed through the mind of the lone ex-airman that day? We shall never know. But we do know that the passing of time, year upon year, must never be allowed to erode the memory of The Gallant Few.

11 July

'In friendship and in service, one to another, we are pledged to keep alive the memory of those of all nations who died in the Royal Air Force and in the Air Forces of the Commonwealth. In their name we give ourselves to this noble cause. Proudly and thankfully we will remember them.'

The RAFA Act of Remembrance.

12 July

If I can let into some soul a little light,
If I some pathway dark and drear can render bright,
If I to one in gloom can show the joyous side,
Though no reward I win, I shall be satisfied.

13 July

Eye hath not seen, nor ear heard, neither have entered into the heart of man, the things which God hath prepared for them that love him.

1 Corinthians 2 : 9.

14 July

I am indebted to the Venerable Paul Wheatley, Archdeacon of Sherborne, for the little story he told when preaching at West Stafford, near Dorchester. It was about the captain of a small boat that was taking a party of actors and actresses to the Shetlands. They were a lively lot from London on tour, and the skipper's insistence on saying Grace before a meal they thought very old-fashioned. A severe storm blew up, and, as the boat began to pitch violently, morale among the passengers got lower and lower. A deputation went to see the skipper. "Maybe we'll get through," he said. "Maybe we won't." As the storm worsened, another deputation went to the captain to ask him to say a prayer with his terrified passengers. His reply was simple: "I say my prayers when it's calm. When it's rough I attend to my ship."

15 July

Today, St. Swithin's Day, is named after the famous Bishop of Winchester who, according to legend, asked when he died he should be buried among the poor outside the cathedral in the churchyard. His wishes were granted, but many years later it was decided to move his body into the cathedral. On the day chosen for the body to be moved – 15 July, 871 – it's said to have rained heavily, and as the rain went on almost continuously for forty days the idea was abandoned. So arose the legend that if it rains on 15 July it will continue to rain for forty days. I'm sure most of us doubt the story very much! But, true or not, it's a much better one, and far more interesting, than many of those we read nowadays in our newspapers. (According to a 19th-century Oxford professor, St. Swithin's remains were eventually moved into the cathedral.)

16 July

Once a railway enthusiast, always a railway enthusiast. That's what they say, and it certainly applies to those keen volunteers who run such lines as the Bluebell, Paignton & Dartmouth, Isle of Wight, West Somerset, and of course Swanage. It was way back in February, 1979, when 'The Swanage Railway Co.' was formed by volunteers, with the aim of buying the track and stations along the old Purbeck branch line. Six months later their first passenger train left Swanage from a temporary platform. Since then, one-million passengers have been carried along the track to Corfe Castle and Norden. That's not the end of the story. On this day – a Saturday, 16 July – in 1994 came what was possibly the company's greatest moment – crowds packed the station to watch the first train to be hauled out of Swanage by the world's most famous locomotive, The Flying Scotsman, on loan from Nene Valley Railway.

Just shows, doesn't it, what can be achieved when enthusiasm is married to determination – and, most important of all, determination is married to dedication.

17 July

> WHEN YOU WERE BORN
> Your parents brought you.
> WHEN YOU WERE MARRIED
> Your spouse brought you.
> WHEN YOU DIE
> Your friends will bring you.
> So – Why not try coming on your own?
> *(On a church notice-board in Scotland!)*

18 July

If God did not forgive, Heaven would be empty.

19 July

You may have heard of the old saying 'If you kill a spider it will rain'. That may or may not be true, but it is certainly true that if you do kill a spider you kill a very useful weather forecaster. A web spun when rain or wind are approaching has its radiating threads much shorter than those spun when dry, calm weather is likely. This is because the spider doesn't want to venture any further than necessary when it's wet and windy outside and damp and draughty indoors. Amazing, isn't it? I often wonder if we really appreciate the common sense and intelligence of so many of the lovely creatures that live around and among us.

> All things bright and beautiful,
> All creatures great and small,
> All things wise and wonderful,
> The Lord God made them all.

20 July

And God spake unto Noah, saying . . . Bring forth with thee every living thing that is with thee, of all flesh, both of fowl, and of cattle, and of every creeping thing that creepeth upon the earth; that they may breed abundantly in the earth, and be fruitful, and multiply upon the earth.
Genesis 8 : 15, 17.

21 July

What a fuss some of us make about trivial things. A friend told me how he had opened a charity garden fete. I reckon he took a good fifteen minutes to explain what he had said in his speech. Some days later a neighbour insisted on telling me in the minutest detail how she had missed her train on the way to Maiden Newton. In striking contrast to my friend and the neighbour, a famous astronaut needed only thirteen words to tell the world of one of the greatest events in world history: "That is one small step for a man; one giant leap for mankind". The astronaut: Neil Armstrong. The time and date: 03.56 BST., Monday 21 July, 1969. The event: man's first landing and walk on the moon. I reckon we can all learn something from Neil Armstrong.

22 July

Two years and five days after Armstrong – on 26 July, 1971 – Colonel James B. Irwin went to the moon on the Apollo 15 mission. The flight had a profound effect on Irwin (who died aged sixty-one, on 8 August, 1991). On his return he said that he had experienced "an overwhelming awareness of God", and later he became a Baptist Minister. "When I climbed down the ladder of the lunar module," he said, "I was really taken aback by the mountains. They seemed so close. They were golden

... Running through my reflections were the words from my favourite biblical passage, from Psalms: 'I will lift up mine eyes unto the hills, from whence cometh my help. My help cometh from the Lord'."

Not for the first time, a brave man, whether on earth or in the heavens, was conscious of that Higher Being in his hour of danger.

23 July

> The noonday sun for glory,
> The quiet of the night for peace;
> In the garden, says the story,
> God walks –
> And His love brings release.

24 July

Remember it is always better to understand a little than to misunderstand a lot.

25 July

I'm sure you know of the poem by A. A. Milne about young Christopher Robin, and the struggle the boy had to concentrate on his prayers. All sorts of things kept coming into his mind. He thought how the water that came out of the hot tap was so hot. And the water that came out of the cold was so cold. Maybe you, too, like Christopher, find it hard to keep your mind on what you are trying to say, especially when you're tired at the end of the day. I know I do. But, later, how glad we are that we didn't give in because it is through prayer that we come to know God, and that is a most wonderful, precious blessing.

26 July

The sun sinks below the distant hills;
Sadly, gently, the last golden ray
Bids farewell to the western world,
And leaves behind another day.

Memories linger, then begin to pale
As surely as the sun's fading light;
Now the heavenly stars shine down
And lead us softly into night.

Let no anxious thoughts disturb your rest,
Nor pain, nor loneliness, nor sorrow;
Peace be yours as you leave to God
The cares of a new tomorrow.

                                               Wayfarer.

27 July

And I say unto you, Ask, and it shall be given you; seek, and ye shall find; knock, and it shall be opened unto you.

                                               St. Luke 11 : 9.

28 July

A few years ago from a shop in Sturminster Newton, in North Dorset, I was given a small paperback entitled 'Michael Parkinson's Confession Album'. The cover explained that it contained the 'intimate confessions of well-known people – John Betjeman, Agatha Christie, Morecambe & Wise, David Niven, etc.' One of the questionnaires had been filled in by the astronomer, Patrick Moore, and against the line 'My ideal virtue' he had written 'Loyalty'. A little word, but with such a big meaning. Oh, for more loyalty these days – to loved ones, to our country, to our principles, to employers, to all things honourable and decent.

29 July

> Remember well, and bear in mind,
> A faithful friend is hard to find;
> > But if you find one good and true,
> > Don't change an old one for a new.

30 July

As far as is known, it's probably the only one in the world – the Chimpanzee Rescue Centre. It was opened about a mile outside Wool, in South Dorset, in the July of 1987. Now there are more than one hundred animals there, including over twenty chimpanzees, together with lemurs, macaques and orangutans. The chimpanzees were rescued from beaches in Spain, where they'd been used by heartless photographers to attract their tourist trade. With the support of the Born Free Foundation and the Great Ape Escape Campaign, the Centre – known as Monkey World – aims to continue its rescue work and bring an end to this cruel trade.

Isn't it amazing how some people will abuse God's creatures for their own selfish gain? Isn't it wonderful, too, that thanks to the rescuers and those who run the Centre, these physically and mentally-abused animals can once more live happily – free in their homely enclosures to roam and climb in complete safety?

31 July

There's so much bad in the best of us, and so much good in the worst of us, that it ill behoves any of us to talk about the rest of us!

August

1 August

> 'Twixt Branksome Chine and Studland
> Lies the entrance to Poole Quay,
> Encompassing a legend
> Of maritime history;
> Salt-ships laden with fish-pots,
> Dried fruit, smooth oil, and wine,
> And contraband from smuggling,
> Were once the cargo's line.
> Yet, close-by are sand-hills
> And gardens that outshine …
> While dolphins weave between the yachts
> Playing in the brine.

2 August

Jesus saith unto him, Thomas, because thou hast seen me, thou hast believed: blessed are they that have not seen, and yet have believed.

St. John 20 : 29.

3 August

I didn't have time; I got up late one morning,
And rushed right into the day . . .
I had so much to accomplish, I didn't have time to pray.
Problems just tumbled about me;
Heavier became each task . . .
"Why doesn't God help me?" I wondered.
He answered, "You didn't ask."
I woke up early this morning, and paused
Before entering the day . . .
I had so much to accomplish that I had to make time to pray.

4 August

What counts is more important than what can be counted.

5 August

I had a friendly smile, I gave that smile away.
The milkman and the postman seemed glad of it each day.
I took it out when shopping, I had it in the street.
I gave it (without thinking) to all I chanced to meet.
I always gave my smile away, as thoughtless as could be,
Yet every time (how wonderfully)
My smile returned to me.

6 August

A happy smile, a cheerful word,
Help make life a joke,
But life's joke is even better
When shared with other folk.

7 August

You'll find them everywhere as the countryside you roam – England's little villages, standing all alone – Tucked away, quiet and still . . . In wooded valley, on distant hill. Lofty barns stacked high with hay – Pastures where the cattle stray – White-washed cottages, thatched and neat . . . The local inn where the menfolk meet. Ancient pump, well-kept green – Church and chapel, winding stream – In each new day each plays its part . . . So precious to each villager's heart.

8 August

We cannot expect anyone to see eye to eye with us if we are looking down on them.

9 August

This is a story about four people: Everybody, Somebody, Anybody, Nobody. There was an important job to be done, and Everybody was sure that Somebody would do it. Anybody could have done it, but Nobody did it. Somebody got angry about that because it was Everybody's job. Everybody thought Anybody could do it, but Nobody realised that Everybody wouldn't do it. It ended up with Everybody blaming Somebody when Nobody did what Anybody could have done.

10 August

If ye do not forgive, neither will your Father which is in heaven forgive your trespasses.

St. Mark 11 : 26.

11 August

Try a little kindness when you want to get things done;
Try a little sympathy for that's how hearts are won;
Try a little gentleness with folk who make you mad,
Maybe then you'll see they're not really half so bad!

12 August

The benefit of telling the truth is you don't have to remember what you said!

13 August

Stored away in my study I have an old Calendar of Quotations. It was compiled by my late Father for the year 1939. For each day there is a small, simple quotation or verse or proverb, suggested (and paid for) by parishioners in my native home town of Melton Mowbray, in Leicestershire. The donations, and the money raised by the sale of the calendar, went to St. Mary's Parish Church, surely one of England's finest parish churches. I have to admit the calendar was partly responsible for the idea behind the compilation of this book. Each quotation bears the name of the person who chose it; this one was my Father's choice:

> Finish thy work, then rest;
> Till then – rest never.
> The rest prepared for thee by God
> Is rest for ever.

How appropriate for today, the anniversary of my dear Father's death in 1962.

14 August

Ideals are like stars: we never reach them, but – like sailors – we can chart our course by them.

15 August

A quotation I noticed in a Sunday newspaper many years ago: 'Life may be compared to a sentence, the meaning of which is clear only when the last word is reached.' A cynic may describe it as just a parting thought, but it contains a large grain of truth.

16 August

> The heavens surely cannot hold
> A sphere so wonderful as ours,
> Splendours created – new and old –
> Were not devised by human powers.
> Panoramic depths and heights
> Of lands and seas – our days and nights –
> Balanced in space, this mystic round
> The sun and moon and stars surround.
>
> Kay Ennals.

17 August

A young student nurse, training at a hospital in Dorset, went into a stationer's shop to buy an urgently-needed textbook. The only copy she could find was very expensive, so she asked an assistant if he had any cheaper shop-soiled copies. "Sorry," he replied. Fighting back tears of disappointment, the young nurse watched the assistant climb a ladder to replace the book on a shelf. Suddenly, the book fell to the ground with a thud. The assistant came down the ladder, picked up the book, and – with the suggestion of a slight smile on his face – said, "This one's shop-soiled. Half price, eh?" An over-joyed trainee nurse left the shop with her book – and a very grateful heart.

18 August

They that sow in tears shall reap in joy.

Psalms 126 : 5.

19 August

Surely there's no finer sight . . . Than a garden in full bloom;
By the brilliant summer sunlight – Or the splendour of the moon.
Ivy climbing weathered wall . . . Tulips stately, standing tall;
Roses boasting deep, rich reds – Pansies nodding golden heads.
Rambler hugging path archway . . . Shallow pond with fish a-play; Birds a-nesting in the trees – Gently swaying in the breeze.
Heavenly perfume fills the air . . . Heavenly colours everywhere; What a dull place Earth would be – Without these gifts, Lord, from Thee.

20 August

It was on this day in 1912 that General William Booth, founder of the Salvation Army, died after a long and painful illness. I remember so vividly, as a teenager in my home-town of Melton Mowbray, listening to the band of The Sallies as they toured the town on Sunday mornings. I knew little then of their good deeds. Now, many years later, I know differently. I have an enormous admiration for their noble work among the poor, the old, the disabled. Every time I see that navy uniform I think of those words of Christ: "Verily I say unto you, In as much as ye have done it unto one of the least of my brethren, ye have done it unto me" . . . Words which can certainly be applied to the Salvation Army.

21 August

A wise old man once said to me,
"Remember as long as you live
"You make your living by what you get,
"But your life by what you give."

22 August

Fed-up with news of wars, violence, riots, strikes, a broadcaster in the Netherlands launched a programme dealing only with good news. It was an immediate success. I can understand why. Many times I've heard my journalistic colleagues proclaim "Bad news is good news". But they are not that stupid and that hardened (well, not most of them) to really mean it. It is surely up to all of us, journalists included, to spread as much good news, as much happiness, as much sunshine, as we can, as often as we can.

23 AUGUST

> Too often dark clouds gather,
> Too often we know sorrow;
> Help me, Lord, to spread your joy
> Yesterday, today – tomorrow!

24 AUGUST

Let the peace of God rule in your hearts.

Colossians 3 : 15.

25 AUGUST

On a visit to Wiltshire, My Beloved and I spent several moments looking up at the great spire of Salisbury Cathedral. It is, of course, the highest spire in England, soaring skywards more than 400-feet above the surrounding water-meadows. It took thirty years to build, and has been proudly standing there since the late 14th century. The second highest spire in England surmounts the Norman tower of another of our lovely cathedrals, Norwich; the weathercock is 315-feet above the ground. What beauty, what majesty, there is in these spires – and in the many others to be found in our land. The wonder of the construction thrills me every time I look at one. And, remember, in the far-off days the men who built them had no cranes, no lifts, no computers. But they most certainly did have a helping-hand . . . the Hand of God.

26 AUGUST

At a school garden fete I bought the 1983 edition of 'The Friendship Book' by Francis Gay – a book published annually by D. C. Thomson (who, incidentally, I worked for as a sub-editor in London and Glasgow). By sheer coincidence, I opened the book at the page where there was 'a thought for 26 August', the date of my birthday. It contained a fascinating anecdote about the late Mahatma Gandhi. He was standing in the doorway of a railway carriage at a station in India, and as the train began to move one of his shoes slipped off and fell on to the track. Gandhi quickly took off his other shoe and dropped that, too, on to the track. Seeing the puzzled look of a fellow-passenger, he said "One shoe wouldn't do much good to a poor man – a pair would."

As 'The Friendship Book' said, it was one of the wonderful things about Gandhi – he saw things in terms of how they affected others. Not a bad guide for life.

27 August

The devil is never afraid of a dust-covered Bible.

28 August

> Fairest to me of all delights
> That makes this earth an heaven,
> Is the joy of finding it's half-past six
> When I thought it was half-past seven!

29 August

Dorset (or Dorsetshire, as some of us like to call it) has every right to be proud of its many historic buildings, ancient forts, and fine castles – among them Corfe, Christchurch, Portland, Nothe, Sherborne and Lulworth. It was on this date, 29 August, way back in 1929, that, sadly, the castle at Lulworth was largely destroyed by fire.

And to the day, sixty-five years later, in 1994, My Beloved and I visited Lulworth again, and our hearts were lifted to see the restoration work being done, with the help of English Heritage. We can't all own a castle, yet happily in this land of ours the vast majority of us have a home, and as the old saying goes 'An Englishman's home is his castle'. How very true.

30 August

If I was asked to list my ten favourite hymns, without doubt one of them would be the lovely 'Amazing Grace'. The author, John Newton, one-time slave trader, wrote to his wife on this day in 1751, and told how he was press-ganged into joining the Navy. 'I forsook God,' he wrote, 'and He left me for a time to follow the way of my own heart!' After many overseas adventures he left the Navy, and eventually returned home to be ordained into the church and became a curate in the small Buckinghamshire town of Olney. There, with William Cowper, in 1779, he published what became known as The Olney Hymns. Newton, after his tremendous experience of conversion, remained always deeply conscious of the amazing grace of God. Hence the hymn, and that lovely third verse:

> Through many dangers, toils and snares,
> I have already come;
> 'Tis grace that brought me safe thus far,
> And grace will lead me home.

31 August

I pray thee, if I have found grace in thy sight, shew me now thy way, that I may know thee.

Exodus 33 : 13.

September

1 September

A short prayer to guide us through the month ahead: 'O Loving Father, keep us ever close to Thee through the hours and days of this month, that in Thee we may find our strength, our faith, our peace.'

2 September

Mrs. G. was a real town lover. So often she had said she disliked the idea of living in the country, "Everybody knowing everybody else's business". Then suddenly, her brother who lived in an isolated hamlet in Dorset, was taken ill. Mrs. G. was called to his bedside. Immediately, on her arrival, she was overwhelmed by the thoughtfulness of the villagers. They had helped to care for her brother until she arrived, they offered to go shopping for her, and they paid regular visits to her brother as he gradually improved. To crown everything, when it was time for Mrs. G. to return home, one of the villagers took her in his car to the nearest railway station, Weymouth. Later, Mrs. G. told a friend how she was quite overcome by everybody's kindness and concern – "Qualities which too often are missing in busy city life."

3 September

Teach us, good Lord, to serve Thee as Thou deservest;
To give and not to count the cost;
To fight and not to heed the wounds;
To toil and not to seek for rest;
To labour and not to ask for any reward;
Save that of knowing that we do Thy will;
Through Jesus Christ our Lord.

Act of Dedication in churches throughout the land, 3 September, 1942 – third anniversary of outbreak of World War II.

4 September

Have you ever thought how many kinds of talk there are? Big talk, little talk, double talk, loud talk, quiet talk, idle chatter, idle gossip, plain speaking... The trouble is, of course, most of our talk doesn't get us anywhere. If only we'd all talk less and do more – what a happier world it would be!

5 September

How little we appreciate, The beauty of a flower – Swinging in the breeze, Drooping in the shower. Each year these precious jewels, Bloom then fade away – Bringing light and happiness . . . To every passing day. Each has a different colour, Painted by God's own hand – Each adding to the glory, Of nature's wonderland. Maybe a sign of tribute, Of friendship or of love – Each a wonder grown on Earth... But sent from Heaven above.

6 September

Talking with a friend during a visit to the delightful Abbotsbury Gardens, I asked her what flower she would choose if she could take only one to a desert island. Without hesitation she replied, "A rose". That would be my choice – My Beloved's, too. It is such a beautiful, colourful, fragrant flower. Her reply reminded me of those two exquisite lines of the poet Richard Trench:

> The ruby long outlasts the scented rose –
> But then the ruby no such fragrance knows.

7 September

It's about this time of the year – late Summer – that we get the best view of the Milky Way, spreading across the night sky from horizon to horizon. The Milky Way is what we call a galaxy – a vast collection of stars giving the appearance of being very close together, although what we see, in fact, is a line-of-sight effect. Travelling at a rate of 186,000 miles per second, it takes nearly four-and-a-half years for light to reach us from the nearest star. Why not go into the garden tonight and see if you can find this galaxy wonder of the heavens? And marvel at the works of God.

8 September

And God made two great lights; the greater light to rule the day, and the lesser light to rule the night; he made the stars also. And God set them in the firmament of the heaven to give light upon the earth . . . And God saw that it was good.

Genesis 1 : 16, 17, 18.

9 September

> Make new friends,
> But keep the old;
> One is silver,
> The other gold.

10 September

> I am only one, But I *am* one.
> I cannot do everything,
> But I *can* do something.
> What I can do, I *ought* to do;
> And what I ought to do
> By the grace of God
> I *will* do.

11 September

The visiting preacher told the story during his sermon in a Dorset village church. At the Golden Gate a parson complained because a motorist, who had been in court for dangerous driving, was allowed to enter before he was. St. Peter smiled and explained, "In 20 minutes on the A25 the motorist woke up and put the fear of God into more people than you did in twenty-five years." A bit naughty, but I like it!

12 September

> Some of us have this world's goods,
> Some of us have none;
> But all of us have got the woods,
> And all have got the sun.
>
> A Canadian lumberjack.

13 September

"No, I don't go to church. Well, hardly ever, but I do pray sometimes if there's something worrying me." . . . "No, I'm not religious, never have been, but when my brother was hurt in a car accident I did say a quick prayer." So often we hear remarks like these. No matter what our beliefs, when we are anxious we usually turn to that higher Heavenly power. Thank goodness we do.

14 September

Whatsoever ye shall ask in my name, that I will do . . . I will not leave you comfortless.

St. John 14 : 13, 18.

15 September – Battle of Britain Day

Fifteenth of September, 1940: According to some historians, the day that changed the course of World War Two – now known as Battle of Britain Day. Post-war official records show that fifty-three German aircraft were destroyed and twenty-two damaged. Over 150 German aircrew were killed or taken prisoner. RAF losses: twenty-six aircraft, thirteen pilots.

"The gratitude of every home in our island, in our Empire, and indeed throughout the world, except in the abodes of the guilty, goes out to the British airmen who, undaunted by odds, unwearied in their constant challenge and mortal danger, are turning the tide of world war by their prowess and by their devotion. Never in the field of human conflict was so much owed by so many to so few."

Winston Churchill.

16 September

What a magnificent cathedral York Minster is. There is so much to see, to study, to praise, to talk about, to thank God for. But as I walked away from it – a few days after the annual Battle of Britain commemoration – I was still reflecting on the words on the RAF Memorial: "They went through air and space without fear, and the shining stars marked their shining deeds."

A fitting tribute indeed to those Gallant Few – and to their brave successors in the conflicts in the Falklands and the Gulf, and in Northern Ireland and the former Yugoslavia.

17 September

It was 17 September, 1944. Parachutes and gliders of the 1st Airborne Division filled the sky over Arnhem. Nearly twelve thousand officers and men landed. After ten days of heroism and horror, more than eight thousand had been killed, wounded, or reported missing. Just over a year later, on 11 November, 1945, a paratrooper went to the Garden of Remembrance outside Westminster Abbey to pay homage to fallen comrades. "Where?" he asked, "is the plot for the Arnhem men?" There wasn't one. The lone 'trooper threw his red beret to the ground, and planted four small wooden crosses. "There is one now," he said, slowly walking away with tears in his eyes.

Here was pride, mingled with grief and remembrance. May we, too, always proudly remember.

18 September

Be thou faithful unto death, and I will give thee a crown of life.

Revelation 2 : 10.

19 SEPTEMBER

Home – what memories that simple word revives,
What pleasures from that castle one derives;
No place on Mother Earth so dear,
A place where friends from far and near
Gather, talk and play.

There we're taught to live a-right,
To strive for justice,
Not for might;
To bear misfortune with a grin,
To exercise the will to win;
To give of our best
Come what may,
And help each other
Along life's way.

20 SEPTEMBER

'O Lord, Thou knowest how busy I must be this day. If I forget Thee, do not forget me' –

> Sir Jacob Astley's prayer before the first Battle of Newbury, 20 September, 1643.

21 SEPTEMBER

September – Time for harvest gathering-in,
Lest the storms and the frosts of Winter begin;
Give thanks for this miracle of the soil,
The annual fruits of the farmer's toil.

22 SEPTEMBER

In some churches at harvest-time specially-made loaves of bread, bearing a pattern of five little loaves and two fishes, are placed on or near the altar. The loaves are there as a reminder of the story in The Good Book which tells how Christ, given the same number of loaves and fishes, blessed them, and with them fed 5,000 people. A miracle we call it. God performs a similar miracle every year. A sack of tiny seeds sown in the Spring becomes a field of corn in the Autumn. A small packet of seeds from Humphries' Garden Centre becomes a row of beans or lettuces in our gardens. Almost as wonderful, isn't it, as the miracle Jesus performed by the sea?

23 SEPTEMBER

The world is full of willing folks: some willing to work, others willing to let them.

24 SEPTEMBER

Somewhere over the brow of the hill
There's an end to strain and strife;
There is peace and hope and promise
Of a good and happy life.
Somewhere over the brow of the hill
There's a place where sunlight gleams,
And golden fields where we all can reap
The harvest of our dreams.

25 SEPTEMBER

I wonder if you have ever heard of the Church of St. Just-in-Roseland? It was on a lovely, warm September day in 1991 that My Beloved and I, on holiday in Cornwall, visited the church, nestling at the end of a creek just a few miles from St. Maws. The church, which attracts thousands of tourists every year, is widely known for its granite stones. Over fifty of them, each with a text or a verse from scripture or from a hymn, line the paths of the beautifully-kept churchyard.

There is a legend which claims that Joseph of Arimathea came to the Fal and brought the boy Jesus with him. During the visit, Jesus landed at St. Just and talked to religious leaders there. It is a persistent legend, it could have happened, and (as the church booklet says) 'It warms the heart to have such a story associated with this lovely place'.

26 SEPTEMBER

> Take a bucket
> And fill it with water,
> Put in your arm
> Up to the wrist;
> Pull it out
> And the hole that is left
> Will be the measure
> Of how much you'll be missed!

27 SEPTEMBER

If a man deceives me once, shame on him; if he deceives me twice, shame on me.

> 18th century Scottish proverb.

28 SEPTEMBER

It is better to trust in the Lord than to put confidence in man ... O give thanks unto the Lord; for He is good: for his mercy endureth for ever.

> Psalms 118 : 8, 29.

29 September

> Faith came singing into my room,
> Other guests took flight;
> Fear and anxiety, grief and gloom
> Sped out into the night.
> I wondered how these things could be;
> Faith gently whispered,
> "Don't you see?
> They really cannot live with me."

30 September

It's growing yellow with the passing of fifteen years, but the Sunday Express cutting in my desk still holds a message for all of us: "What a terrifying journey it must have been for the three Rumanian families who escaped to the West in a single-engine biplane. For 250 miles they huddled in the ancient aircraft as it flew across Rumanian and Hungarian territory at tree-top level to avoid radar. Finally . . . they made a hair-raising emergency landing in an Austrian field. There may be plenty to grumble about here in Britain. But do we not have something to learn from those who would risk their lives for that priceless blessing we so often take for granted? Freedom."

October

1 October

On this first day of a new month let us thank God for all those dear to us who have departed this life in His faith and fear, beseeching Him to give us grace so to follow their good example, that, this life ended, we may dwell with Him and them in life everlasting.

2 October

There is a home that lies beyond,
And past its golden door
Awaits the one who's gone away,
Not lost – Just gone before.

3 October

Do not stand at my grave and weep,
I am not here, I do not sleep.
I am the sunlight on ripened grain,
I am gentle autumnal rain and the soft stars that shine at night.
Do not stand at my grave and cry,
I am not here, I did not die.

Words written by a soldier of the Royal Artillery on his posting to Ulster, and sent in an envelope to his home at Cosham to be opened in the event of his death. In October, 1989, he was killed by a landmine near Londonderry.

4 October

Are life's worries always on your mind? – Are the quiet moments difficult to find? – Then seek the open spaces, 'neath the open sky . . . The open fields where the winds go by. Go seek the woods where the bluebells grow – The hills and valleys where the streams gently flow – Listen to the song of the birds as they play . . . Breathe in the fragrance of the new sweet hay. Seek the peace of the still country lane – The warmth of the sun, the freshness of the rain – Rest in the cool, gathering shade . . . Find new strength 'midst Nature's Parade.

5 October

A new commandment I give unto you, That ye love one another; as I have loved you, that ye also love one another.
St. John 13 : 34.

6 October

As I upon my road did pass
A school-house back in May
There out upon the beaten grass
Wer maidens at their play;
An' as the pretty souls did tweil
An' smile, I cried, 'The flow'r
O' beauty, then, is still in bud
In Blackmwore by the Stour.'

William Barnes, 1801-1886.
Dorset philologist, poet,
one-time curate at Winterborne Whitcombe
and Rector of Winterborne Came,
who died 6/7 October.

7 October

> When the One Great Scorer comes to write
> against your name,
> He marks – not that you won or lost,
> but – how you played the game.
>> Grantland Rice, US author, 1880-1954.

8 October

Over the years, millions of people have joined in the special weeks of prayer for world peace. "If only we could have peace everywhere – everywhere," said a Dorset veteran of the Royal Navy. An impossible dream? So it seems. But it's good for us to remember that, whereas today there are millions of believers the world over, not so very long ago there was just Jesus – with twelve followers.

An impossible dream?

9 October

> Far beyond, where are no storms,
> And human worries cease,
> And time and space are both unknown,
> We'll find God's perfect peace.

10 October

> Does it matter one has wisdom,
> Another, not one grain?
> Perhaps the longing of the soul
> Unlatches the door to fame.
>> Kay Ennals.

11 October

When next you pray remember – The victims of war, Remember those we love – And those we see no more. Remember the sick and homeless – Those torn apart, The lonely and the aged – Those of broken heart. Remember our allies – Those striving at our side, Our monarch, our leaders – Those called upon to guide. Above all else remember – In the quiet evening hour . . . 'Tis God and God alone – Who commands the greatest power.

12 October

Thou wilt keep him in perfect peace, whose mind is stayed on thee: because he trusteth in thee.

Isaiah 26 : 3.

13 October

It was an elderly gentleman at Ferndown who first mentioned the quotation to me: 'Our necessities are few, but our wants are endless'. How very, very right he was.

14 October

Deck-chairs are stored away in the shed, cricket bats and pads in the loft, bathing costumes in the cupboard. Summer has gone again. But think of the consolations. Jars of home-grown raspberries and gooseberries load kitchen shelves. Leaves from the trees begin to form a golden carpet in the lane. Thoughts turn to buttered toast round glowing embers. And the air is fresh and crisp as only Autumn air can be. Yes, Autumn is here again and with all its joys and wonders, who really cares that Summer is just a memory?

15 October

As Manager of BBC Radio Solent from its opening day in 1970 to 1978, it was essential that I listened to as much of the output as time allowed. And I recall clearly on this day in 1973 listening to the daily 'Morning Thought'. It was given by a company director from Alresford, in Hampshire, and in it he quoted the famous Time poem, a framed copy of which is attached to a clock in Chester Cathedral.

> When as a child I laughed and wept,
> Time crept.
> When as a youth I waxed more bold,
> Time strolled.
> When I became a full-grown man,
> Time ran.
> When older still I daily grew,
> Time flew.
> Soon I shall find, in passing on,
> Time gone.
> O Christ! Wilt thou have saved me then?

16 October

Time past cannot be recalled.

> 14-century proverb.

17 October

It was in 1969 that a Sanctuary for Donkeys was started by Dr. Elisabeth Svendsen at Ottery St. Mary, in Devon. Within a few years the demands on the sanctuary were so great that more acreage was needed, and the charity moved to Sidmouth. Twenty-six years on, the sanctuary has taken through its gates 6,000 donkeys – some of them cruelly treated, others abandoned, and some whose owners could no longer look after them. They included Islander, abandoned for eighteen years on an island off Ireland . . . Timothy whose ears were slashed by vandals . . . and Blackie who was rescued from a cruel fiesta in Spain. The sanctuary has a fully-equipped hospital, and after a stay of a few weeks some of the donkeys – provided they are fit – go to one of the charity's outlying farms.

There's a saying that charity begins at home. True or not, it certainly can be found, in abundance, at this 'home' for these wonderful little creatures.

18 OCTOBER

Are not five sparrows sold for two farthings, and not one of them is forgotten before God.

St. Luke 12 : 6.

19 OCTOBER

A home to love,
And a garden to tend,
Makes the dawning a joy,
And the sunset a friend.

20 OCTOBER

The world will never adjust itself
To suit your whims to the letter.
Some things go wrong your whole life long,
And the sooner you know it the better.

21 October

England expects that every man will do his duty.
Nelson's famous signal,
Battle of Trafalgar, 21 October, 1805.

22 October

There was another signal flown from Nelson's flagship on the day before the battle. The coxswain of HMS Victory had been so busy preparing the final mailbags that he forgot his own letter to his wife. Nelson ordered a signal to bring back the mailboat for, as he said, there was no knowing if the next day might be the coxswain's last. An historic, thoughtful gesture on an historic occasion. Thoughtful gestures we make towards others in our everyday, humdrum life may not be as historic, but they are still just as worthwhile – and the impact on the receiver may be just as great as it must have been on the wife of the HMS Victory coxswain.

23/24 October –

Anniversary of the Battle of Alamein, 1942

'The battle will be one of the decisive battles of history. It will be the turning point of the war . . . Let every officer and man enter the battle with a stout heart, and with the determination to do his duty so long as he has breath in his body . . . Let us all pray "the Lord mighty in battle" will give us the victory' – General Montgomery's eve-of-battle message to his troops. Victory it certainly was. One of the turning points in the war it certainly was. On this anniversary day of the second Battle of Alamein let us remember the cost: after ten days of fighting, 2,350 allied lives lost and 11,200 wounded or missing.

24 October

I am persuaded, that neither death, nor life, nor angels, nor principalities, nor powers, nor things present, nor things to come, Nor height, nor depth, nor any other creature, shall be able to separate us from the love of God, which is in Christ Jesus our Lord.

Romans 8 : 38, 39.

25 October

The kindness we neglect today may be a bitter regret tomorrow.

26 October

> He wore a crown of thorns,
> He endured the cross of strife;
> Now he sits on God's right-hand,
> And wears a crown of life.

27 October

Character: the only thing we make in this world which we can take with us into the next.

28 October

Thomas Hardy, at his home at Max Gate, Dorchester, wrote in October, 1900, that he had been 'on a little cycle tour'. He had ridden 'to Upwey, where there is a wishing well. We duly wished, and what will result remains to be seen'. He was referring, of course, to the now famous Upwey Wishing Well. Legend has it that the spring, close by the village Church of St. Lawrence, first became known as a wishing well about 1857. Nowadays, some

10,000 people a year come to fill a little cup from the well, sip the water, make a wish, and then over their left shoulder throw the rest of the water back into the well to join the River Wey on its five-mile journey to Weymouth and the sea. How often wishes come true, I know not! But I do know there's a quiet, peaceful magic surrounding the well, and if your wish comes true that's an added bonus! Life's like that, isn't it? We all have our own private wishes and hopes, and then – as Hardy said – 'What will result remains to be seen'.

29 October

Great issues call for great courage, and great courage brings great rewards.

Lord Tebbit.

30 October

It was at the end of October a few years ago that a visiting minister, Canon Hugh Mumford, preached about faith at our village Church of St. Andrew in West Stafford. He told an intriguing story about a famous tightrope-walker who crossed the Niagra Falls in Canada. After completing his dangerous walk, the performer asked an onlooker if he thought he could cross again, this time pushing a wheelbarrow. "Yes," replied the onlooker. Replied the performer, "Jump in!" Inevitably, the spectator declined. That really was too much of a test for his faith. So often we, too, express our faith in something – but how genuine and sincere is it when it is really put to the test?

31 October

Try to keep your face always towards the sun, and the shadows will fall behind you.

November

1 November

> It's easy enough to be pleasant
> When life flows by like a song,
> But the one worthwhile
> Is the one who will smile
> When everything goes wrong.

2 November

> Let not your heart be troubled; ye believe in God, believe also in me.
>
> St. John 14 : 1.

3 November

> When I'm feeling lonely, I'll always think of you;
> Do not despair, my love, we'll see it through.
> Though we must be apart, memories remain;
> I'll always be faithful, 'til we kiss again.

4 November

A large notice seen outside a church in Weymouth: 'Come in and have your faith lifted.' Pretty good advice!

5 November

The loveliest things in life are the things you cannot buy:
The ripple of a stream, the stars in the sky,
The song of the birds, the setting of the sun,
The rest and the peace, when the day is done.

6 November

'Please God give me work till my life shall end, and life till my work is done.' These seventeen words were written in the front of my late Father's prayer-book which faithfully he carried to church each Sunday.
God granted his wish. Is it our wish, too?

7 November

Did you know that in the Holy Bible – The Good Book, as I like to call it – there are sixty-six books, 1,187 chapters, 31,173 verses, and 773,746 words? And it's the most popular book in the world, some 50,000,000 being distributed each year. If you read one hundred words each day, it will take you 7,737 days – in other words, 1,101 weeks or just twenty-one years – to read right through from Genesis to Revelation. I know, I've done it. Why don't you start now? Before it's too late!

8 November

St. John Ambulance volunteers in Dorset spent over 75,000 hours in one year serving others. Red Cross workers, too, I'm sure, strived in similar fashion. The same, noble example of service by these good folk can be seen throughout the land. Here, undoubtedly, is one 'national debt' that can never, never be repaid.

9 NOVEMBER

By love serve one another.

Galatians 5 : 13.

10 NOVEMBER

> When the golden sun is sinking,
> And your mind from care is free,
> While of others you are thinking,
> Will you spare a thought for me?

11 NOVEMBER – The 'Old' Armistice Day

> Proudly they answered Flander's call
> And paid life's greatest price of all;
> Let us this day those gallant dead
> And all the precious blood they shed –
> Remember.

> Great was their task, their victory,
> Their lives they gave to keep us free;
> In tribute to the bravery
> Of that now silent company,
> May we always – Remember.

12 NOVEMBER

After the First World War an Army padre, the Reverend David Railton, MC, persuaded the British Government to follow the example of France in honouring the dead. A serviceman's body was chosen from four battlefields; then, wrapped in a Union Flag, it was enclosed in a casket of English oak, brought across the Channel in the destroyer Verdun, and on 11 November, 1920, was reburied in Westminster Abbey in soil brought from Ypres. Not many years later it became the symbol of the dead of another World War. Now, each November on Remembrance Sunday, Flanders poppies are laid on the grave of this brave man – The Unknown Warrior.

13 NOVEMBER

In November a few years ago My Beloved and I visited the beautiful city of Norwich – and who could go to Norwich without spending a few, quiet moments in the majestic Parish Church of St. Peter Mancroft? The church, which straddles the ancient market-place like a great ship at anchor, has few rivals among the parish churches of this country (certainly one rival is the fine Church of St. Mary in my native town of Melton Mowbray).

John Wesley wrote of St. Peter Mancroft, 'I scarcely remember ever to have seen a more beautiful parish church; the more so because its beauty results not from foreign ornaments, but from the very fine form and structure of it . . .' How right Wesley was. There is a peaceful serenity, too, about St. Peter Mancroft – a peace and serenity which contrasts sharply with the busy, noisy market-place outside. Such peace and bustle is typical, isn't it, of our lives? And it's the contrast that makes each experience so worthwhile.

14 NOVEMBER

I wonder if you have heard of the apostle Matthias? There is, I believe, only one brief mention of him in The Good Book, in Acts of the Apostles. Soon after the ascension of Christ, a meeting of His followers was held. They decided to elect a successor to Judas Iscariot, who had betrayed Jesus. According to the first chapter of Acts, the followers 'gave forth their lots; and the lot fell upon Matthias; and he was numbered with the eleven apostles'. Little more is known about Matthias, as indeed little is known about many saints. This surely applies, too, to most of the saints we meet in our everyday lives; they are all around us if only we'd take the trouble to look.

15 NOVEMBER

Be ye therefore merciful, as your Father also is merciful.
St. Luke 6 : 36.

16 NOVEMBER

Though a man may conquer a thousand men in battle, a greater conqueror still is he who conquers himself.

17 NOVEMBER

Every day loved ones are torn apart,
Everywhere you find the lonely heart;
Son and sweetheart called from home
To face the outside world alone.

Proudly you wait for his return;
Till then believe, have faith, stand firm.
Then joy will take the place of sorrow
When he returns – maybe tomorrow!

18 NOVEMBER

It's surprising, isn't it, how one learns things when one least expects to? It was a bitter November Sunday, with snow on the ground when I took our little yorkie for his morning walk. Along the street Mr. B. was sweeping the snow from his gate. Then a church bell began tolling.
"I used to be a bell-ringer," said Mr. B. "Campanology, the science of bell-ringing. Taken from the name of the

Italian town, Campania, where the modern church-bell originated." In spite of the cold north wind, Mr. B. went into some detail about the history of bell-ringing... how the modern church bell was introduced into Britain about 600 AD, and how in pre-First-World-War days there were something like 50,000 bell-ringers. "It isn't the same these days, is it?" concluded Mr. B. "The bells still toll, but too often they're ignored. What a better place the world would be if more of us heeded their call."

I continued my walk in quiet thought. The last few words of Mr. B., bless him, made the best mini-sermon I'd heard for a very long time.

19 November

Hours fly,
Flowers die,
Children cry,
Bereaved sigh,
Love stays.

20 November

There must be very few, if any, of us who have never sung that beautiful hymn, 'Abide with me'. It was on an August evening in Devon, in 1847, that life's problems hung heavily on the shoulders of the Vicar of All Saints' Church, Lower Brixham, the Reverend Henry Francis Lyte. He had been Vicar for over twenty years, and had won the hearts of his parishioners. Now, although only fifty-four, he knew his health was failing. In the fading evening light, he looked across the waters of Brixham Harbour. It was a scene he loved so much. Then, returning home to his study, he wrote and wrote and the words flowed. So was created that majestic hymn. Less than a month later Henry Lyte preached his last sermon at Brixham. On 20 November 1847 he died.

On that August evening it must have been the thought that he would not often again look out to sea from his beloved Brixham Harbour, that inspired him to pen the beautiful last verse:

Hold thou thy Cross before my closing eyes;
Shine through the gloom, and point me to the skies;
Heav'n's morning breaks, and earth's vain shadows flee;
In life, in death, O Lord, abide with me.

21 NOVEMBER

Life is a book of volumes three,
The past, the present, the yet to be;
The past is finished and laid away,
The present we are living day by day;
But the third and last of the volumes three
Is hidden away, God holds the key.

22 NOVEMBER

Yes, I know the feeling. You've had a rotten day. Everything seems to have gone wrong. You've been on your feet from the moment you got up. At breakfast you burned the toast. You knocked over a bottle of milk. Then, when you went to the cobblers in the pouring rain to collect your shoes, he was closed. By bedtime, worn and weary, you were thankful the day was over. You were right at the end of your resources. But remember, dear friend, that is just the time when God is only at the beginning of his. Hand over your burdens to him . . .

23 NOVEMBER

Trust in the Lord with all thine heart; and lean not unto thine own understanding.
Proverbs 3 : 5.

24 November

> My little dog – would that she were here
> For me to take to the fields each day,
> As once I did
> To let her play . . .
> My little dog could, with bounding, clear
> Tall meadow grass, and race in wild array,
> But not today.
> Sadly, she's gone away.
>
> Kay Ennals.

25 November

You cannot climb the ladder of success with your hands in your pockets.

26 November

Does the name Sister Dora mean anything to you? Her full name was Dorothy Pattison. She was the daughter of a Yorkshire rector, and worked as a nurse at a hospital in Walsall. But the people of Walsall were very suspicious of newcomers in those days – just over one hundred years ago – and one day a boy threw a stone at Sister Dora, cutting her head. Soon after this ugly incident, the same boy was injured in an accident, and was taken to the hospital where Sister Dora worked. As the days passed he recognised the Sister, and expressed his amazement at the devoted care she had given him. For the first time in his life the boy had met someone who returned good for evil. After this, opposition in Walsall to Sister Dora turned to love, and when she died local people erected a memorial which, I'm told, can still be seen.
Oh, for more Sister Doras . . .

27 November

Prosperity is like a magnet; it draws friends. Adversity is like a refining furnace; it proves them.

28 November

Oh, Jesus, I wish we knew
Why loved ones have to die;
It's hard for us to understand,
No matter how we try.

There must be reasons, Jesus,
But only you know why;
It's not for us to question,
Why loved ones have to die.

29 November

Death is nothing at all. I have only slipped away into the next room... Whatever we were to each other, that we still are. Call me by my old familiar name, speak to me in the easy way which you always used. Life means all that it ever meant. It is the same as it ever was... Why should I be out of mind because I am out of sight? I am waiting for you, for an interval, somewhere very near, just round the corner. All is well.

Henry Scott Holland (1847-1918).
Former Canon, St. Paul's Cathedral.

30 November – St. Andrew's Day

Scotland's patron saint
Was first chosen from the few,
And always will be honoured by
The white cross on the blue.

K. E. E.

December

1 December

> Cold December brings the snow,
> Christmas fun and warm fire glow.

2 December

As we enter the last month of another year I recall so vividly the friend who, whenever she referred to an elderly person, insisted, "Going downhill, you know. Has been for a year or so . . . " Well, more often than not we didn't know. And I dislike the phrase, anyway. The path of life, as we get older, frequently seems to lead uphill rather than downhill. But that's not the point. Surely, as each year passes it is rather like climbing up a hillside, out of a valley. We can look back and see the green pastures and the dark crevices we have passed through. What lies ahead, over the brow of the hill, we know not. All we can do is trust and believe, and place ourselves in the care of God. As a famous old hymn reminds us:

> I shall not fear the battle
> If thou art by my side,
> Nor wander from the pathway
> If thou wilt be my guide.

3 December

The present is always taking us by surprise because we do not sufficiently consider the past.

G. M. Trevelyan.

4 December

I'm sure that at some time or other most of us use the phrase 'Hobson's choice', but how many of us know how it originated? Many years ago, a certain Thomas Hobson set up business near Cambridge as a carrier and also hired out horses. He was very fond of animals, and placed each horse on a sort of rota; this meant that when a customer arrived to collect a horse he/she had to accept the one nearest to the entrance of the yard. Thus, every animal got adequate rest as well as adequate exercise. Hobson refused to break this rule, and so the expression 'Hobson's choice' came into everyday use. You accepted what you were offered, and if you didn't like it that was just too bad! In other words, you had no choice.

Today, over 300 years after his death, the phrase is a lasting memorial to a kindly man who insisted on kindness to his beloved animals. And a street in Cambridge, I'm told, bears his name.

5 December

It's so often true, isn't it, how a little act of kindness, no matter how small, brings another kindness in return? I'm reminded of an old story about four young people in Hastings who had spent nearly all evening trying to collect rummage articles for a local fishermen's charity, known as The Winkle Club. They hadn't been very successful. Then they came to Mrs. B.'s home. Mrs. B. was over seventy, a widow, crippled with arthritis. She went to

enormous trouble to find a few old items. At last, the collectors' evening was beginning to look worthwhile. Five days later, after the sale, there was a knock on Mrs. B.'s door. The young people had returned – this time, to give something . . . a small box of chocolates. "In appreciation," they said, "for the trouble you took last week."
Just a little gesture, but it meant a lot to Mrs. B. – and the young people, I'm sure, found happiness in their giving.

6 December

Freely ye have received, freely give.
St. Matthew 10 : 8.

7 December

If you are in the north of England, in the lovely area of Northumbria, try to find time to visit Holy Island, just off the east coast. Holy Island – or Lindisfarne as it's often called – has an amazing christian history. It began with the arrival of St. Aidan from Iona around the year 635. A missionary and educational centre was started. Then, the great St. Cuthbert was associated with the island, and the famous manuscript known as the Lindisfarne Gospels was written in his honour. The manuscript is now in the British Museum. Holy Island is still a centre of pilgrimage. Do go there if you can – and thank God for the work and witness of those good, saintly people so many years ago.

8 December

We must use time as a tool, not as a couch.
President John F. Kennedy, December 1961.

9 December

I'm thankful to say it didn't happen in Dorset, or in any of our neighbouring counties, but I'm assured it did occur further north, in Cambridgeshire. A customer in a bookshop failed to find any religious publications, so asked an assistant for help. Came the reply, "Because of Christmas, Sir, we've had to move them down to the bottom shelf."

Clearly, a case of *No room in the shop* ... Typical of our times, eh?

10 December

Today – do we really have to remind ourselves? – is the anniversary of the sinking of the battleship Prince of Wales and the battle-cruiser Repulse in a Japanese air attack in 1941. The ships were attacked in the South China Sea after sailing from Singapore with four destroyers to resist Japanese landings in north-east Malaya. Of the 3,092 men in the two ill-fated ships, over 760 were lost. How appropriate today to recall a few lines from W. Whiting's famous hymn 'For those at sea':

> Eternal Father, strong to save,
> Whose arm hath bound the restless wave,
> Who bidd'st the mighty ocean deep
> Its own appointed limits keep;
> O hear us when we cry to Thee
> For those in peril on the sea.

11 December

I am indebted to a parish magazine in Dorset for these little verses, part of a poem which made its way to England from a Methodist Church in South Africa:

> I carry a cross in my pocket,

> A simple reminder to me
> Of the fact that I am a christian
> No matter where I may be.
> When I put my hand in my pocket
> To bring out a coin or a key,
> The cross is there – a reminder
> Of the price He paid for me.

12 December

I cut out the quotation from an old 1939 calendar. Printed against the date 12 December were these words: 'Be pleasant until 10 o'clock in the morning. The rest of the day will take care of itself.' True words indeed! So often we wake up in the morning feeling a little 'under the weather', or perhaps tired after a restless night. And then, hastily, we say something which later we regret. All of us, I am sure, could make the early mornings happier for others and for ourselves if we remember that little quotation.

13 December

A friend assured me of the truth of a Christmas shopping story she had heard. The girl at the cash-register of a shop was checking a customer's purchases. She pressed down the 'total' button, but nothing happened. Then she thumped the register with her fist. The customer asked, "What is going to break first, your wrist or the register?" Replied the girl, "I hope my wrist – then I can claim compensation!" And she probably meant it. Amazing, isn't it, how sometimes we get our priorities wrong?

14 December

Watch therefore: for ye know not what hour your Lord doth come.

St. Matthew 24 : 42.

15 December

Nearly 150 years ago, in a house in London, a little boy lay gravely ill with diptheria. His grief-stricken parents sat by his bedside, and as the doctor looked at the father they were convinced death was close. Miraculously, the boy survived. What a blessing he did – for his name was Thomas John Barnardo, the founder of Dr. Barnardo's Homes in 1866. There is no need for me here to dwell on the wonderful work done since then by Barnardo's. But how appropriate at this time of year, as we prepare for Christmas, to spare a grateful thought for all such societies, including the voluntary ones: Samaritans, WRVS, Help the Aged, CAB, Cancer Relief, Children's Society, ex-service organisations, and so on. It isn't only at Christmas that they bring help and relief, comfort and support, guidance and happiness. Our thanks to each and every one of them.

16 December

Christmas, it's so often said, is a time for children. I say it's a time for adults, too – for Mums and Dads, Aunts and Uncles, Grannies and Grandads. As the greetings-cards, with their robins and holly, come dropping through the letter-box, they bring with them nostalgic reminders of loved ones probably not seen for a long time, of old friends, and of previous neighbours. Each year, as we read the simple, loving, friendly messages, memories come flooding back. Christmas may have its origin in a pagan festival, but we can thank our Heavenly Father that the early christians adopted it as one of the most important dates in their yearly calendar.

17 December

Serenity is not freedom from the storm, but peace amid the storm.

18 December

Few visitors to Dorchester, even if they 'pass by on the other side' can fail to notice the town centre Parish Church of St. Peter. But how many, I wonder, notice the large, diamond-shaped plaque in the 15th-century porch? It explains that under the porch lies buried the Reverend John White, MA, 'born at Christmas 1575', for about forty years Rector of the parish and also of Holy Trinity, and who died on 21 July 1648. A famous puritan, John White was one of the founders of the colony of Massachusetts, New England, where settlers were able to worship freely, and where (according to the plaque) 'his Name lives in unfading Remembrance'.

Time and again we are told we should not dwell on the past, but surely it's well worthwhile occasionally turning back the pages of time. There is much we can learn from men like John White, 'a Man of great Godliness . . . and wonderful Ability and Kindness'.

19 December

The old year is nearly over and done with – or is it? Few things are more alive in our minds than the past; nothing influences our motives and actions more than the past. All of us would surely agree that we can face the future with more confidence if we are prepared to learn from days – and experiences – now gone by. If we are to progress happily and successfully along the highway of life, our New Year resolutions need only Old Year recollections.

20 December

> May God bless every little thing
> Upon a Winter's night;
> All those that are hunted,
> And in fear have taken flight.
> May God bless every little thing
> And guard it in His light,
> For Jesus was a little thing
> Upon a Winter's night.

21 December

Behold, a virgin shall be with child, and shall bring forth a son, and they shall call his name Emmanuel, which being interpreted is, God with us.

St. Matthew 1 : 23.

22 December

The newspaper editorial I read some years ago struck, I thought, just the right note for this week before Christmas: 'As we pull the crackers will it not be the non-material things which stand out as the highlights . . . for Christmas is about the nativity play in the school-hall . . the cheerful thump of a Salvation Army Band . . . and the bright-eyed excitement of youngsters. Above all, it is about the faith and the hope of those millions all over the world who will be in church to sing the carols and hear the old, familiar story of Joseph and Mary, the shepherds and the wise men. And who will once again feel themselves uplifted and at peace, because of the miracle of that event all those years ago in the stable at Bethlehem.'

23 December

The approach of New Year's Eve reminds me of the amazing recovery of a lost ear-ring below Big Ben in London. My Beloved and I had been celebrating, with thousands of other revellers, the arrival of another new year, 1949. As we reached Westminster underground station on our way home, My Beloved suddenly realised she had lost a much-valued ear-ring. In pouring rain, we walked back to Big Ben – more in hope than expectation – and there, lying in the gutter, sparkling in the rain, below the feet of the revellers, was the ear-ring!

What a lovely, lovely start to the New Year. May you, dear reader, also have a lovely start to your New Year.

24 December

It was Christmas Eve, 1918, and in the Austrian village of Oberndarf a local priest, the Reverend Joseph Mohr, had composed the words of a carol. He would have dearly liked it played that evening, but he had no tune for it. Joseph's organist, Franz Gruber, came to the rescue. "I shall compose one now," he said, "and at midnight the hymn shall be sung." Hardly had the service begun when the organ broke down. Franz fetched his guitar, and to its accompaniment the hymn was sung. Later, when the organ-repairer asked for a tune to be played to test the organ, Franz chose the newly-written carol. The repairer and his daughters, who gave concerts, added the hymn to their repertoire. Its popularity rapidly spread. Today, people throughout the world are singing the carol . . . 'Silent night, Holy night'.

Certainly it is one of my favourite carols – possibly the one I love best of all. Thank you, Joseph Mohr and Franz Gruber.

25 December – Christmas Day

> *And the Angel said . . . 'Behold, I bring you good tidings of great joy, which shall be to all people.'*
> St. Luke 2 : 10.

26 December – Boxing Day

Boxing Day! The derivation of the term 'boxing' is in some doubt. It may come from the custom many years ago of the opening of church boxes to give the contents to the poor on the day after Christmas. Another suggestion is that this was the day on which people used to go round collecting their Christmas 'box' for work done during the year. Whatever the derivation, we should remember more importantly that this day is the Feast of St. Stephen, the first christian martyr. He was stoned to death about 33 AD. His stoning, it's said, was watched by Saul, later converted to become St. Paul. As we enjoy ourselves today round the Christmas tree, let us pause for a moment to remember Stephen. Maybe, like Paul, we still need converting . . .

27 December

The hour was late, The world in silence slept;
The shepherds by their flocks, Their nightly vigil kept;
When unto them an angel came, And wise men saw afar,
Before them in the east – A bright, guiding star.
To Bethlehem, They quickly made their way;
And there in a stable, A manger-bed of hay, They saw a
child, In swaddling clothes – An infant newly born,
Bringing to all mankind . . . The first Christmas morn.

28 December

And the shepherds returned, glorifying and praising God for all the things that they had heard and seen, as it was told unto them.

St. Luke 2 : 20.

29 December

I wonder if you recall, as I do, the school-day thrill of a brand new exercise-book? How carefully we wrote our name at the front, how carefully we wrote on the first page, and drew the first lines. Next year lies before us like a brand new exercise-book. How worthy will the words be that we write on each page? As month follows month, and season follows season, will we maintain the standards we are hoping to set ourselves? We can but try and, with God's help, surely we shall succeed.

30 December

Ring out the old,
Ring in the new;
Ring out the false,
Ring in the true.

31 December

When BBC Radio Solent opened in Southampton on New Year's Eve, 1970, the hymn 'O God, our help in ages past' was the inspiration for the station's call-sign. As Solent's Manager, I had the privilege of explaining to listeners that we had based the call-sign on the first five notes of the hymn, which were then adapted radiophonically. The signal, lasting only a few seconds, was taken from a recording of the hymn, which has now been played electronically from the clock-tower of Southampton Civic Centre every day for nearly sixty years.

Radio Solent's choice could not have been more appropriate. The words of the hymn were written by Isaac Watts who was born in Southampton; the signal was used for the first time on the last day of a year; and the final verse looks to the years ahead:

> O God, our help in ages past,
> Our hope for years to come,
> Be thou our guard while troubles last,
> And our eternal home.

Words which, surely, will make up many a silent thought in the days before us.

About the Author...

Maurice Ennals entered journalism in his home town of Melton Mowbray in Leicestershire, and after two years' war service in the RAFVR, worked in Fleet Street and Glasgow. In 1944 he joined the news staff of the BBC, and in 1967 became the first Manager of the Corporation's first local radio station – in Leicester; three years later he opened Radio Solent in Southampton.

Throughout his journalistic career, Maurice Ennals was closely involved in association football – both as player and coach – and on leaving the BBC in 1979 joined AFC Bournemouth as Chief Scout. He later took up the same post with Colchester United; and then spent five years covering the Dorset area for West Bromwich Albion. He now scouts for Shrewsbury Town.

His first book was Sunshine and Showers, a collection of poems, written jointly with his wife, Kay, and published in July, 1987.

A simple prayer to guide us through the New Year:

Give us, O Lord, so firm a faith in your Fatherly love and wisdom, that we may be lifted above our anxieties and fears, and face each day, and the unknown future, with a courageous and quiet spirit.